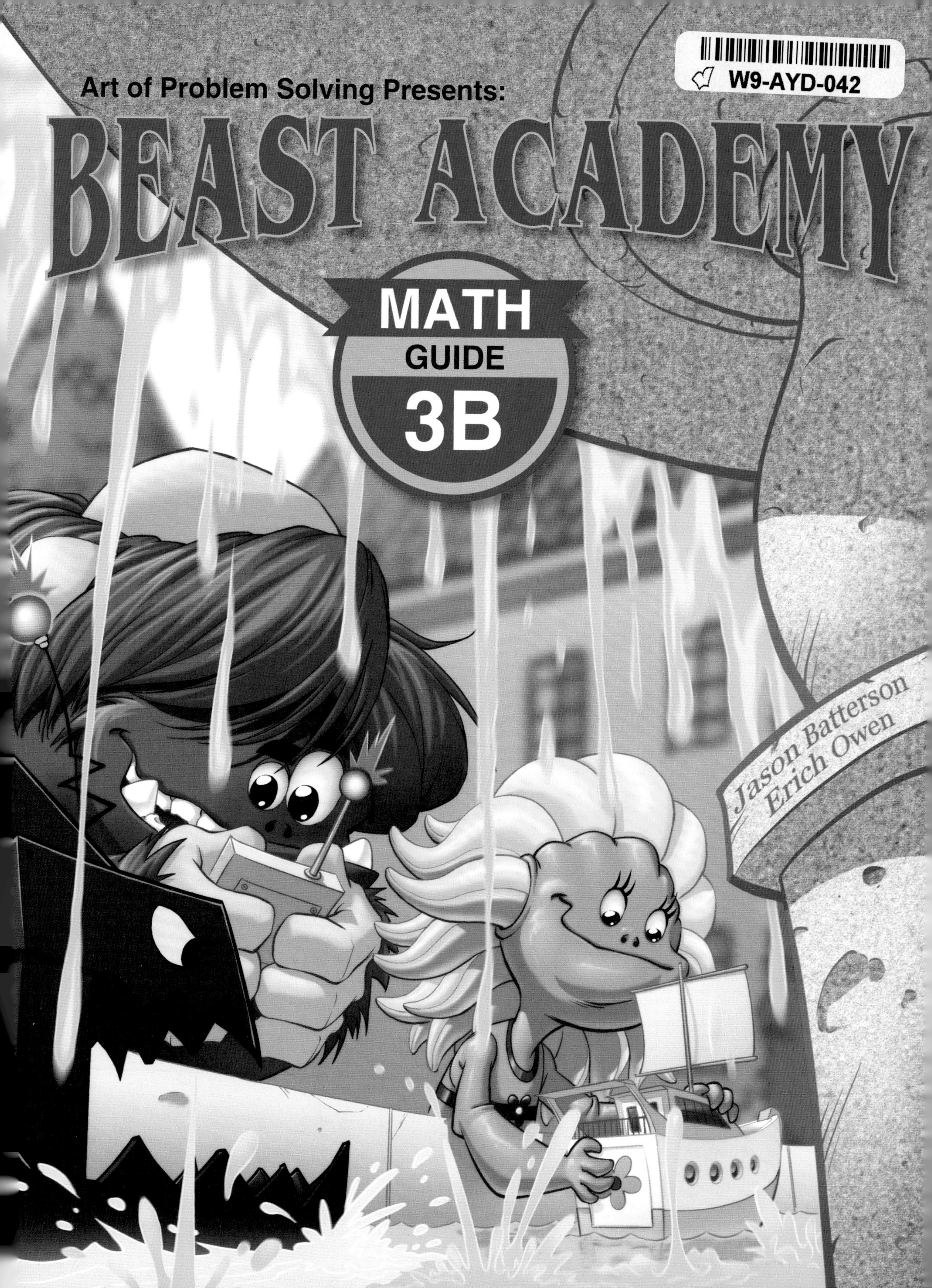
W9-AYD-042
Art of Problem Solving Presents:
BEAST ACADEMY
MATH
GUIDE
3B
Jason Batterson
Erich Owen

Published by: AoPS Incorporated
10865 Rancho Bernardo Rd Ste 100
San Diego, CA 92127-2102
info@BeastAcademy.com

ISBN: 978-1-934124-42-0

Written by Jason Batterson
Illustrated by Erich Owen
Colored by Greta Selman
Cover Design by Lisa T. Phan

Visit the Beast Academy website at www.BeastAcademy.com.
Visit the Art of Problem Solving website at www.artofproblemsolving.com.
Printed in the United States of America.
Second Printing 2015.

Become a Math Beast!
For additional books,
printables, and more, visit

www.BeastAcademy.com

This is Guide 3B in a four-book series for third grade:

Contents:

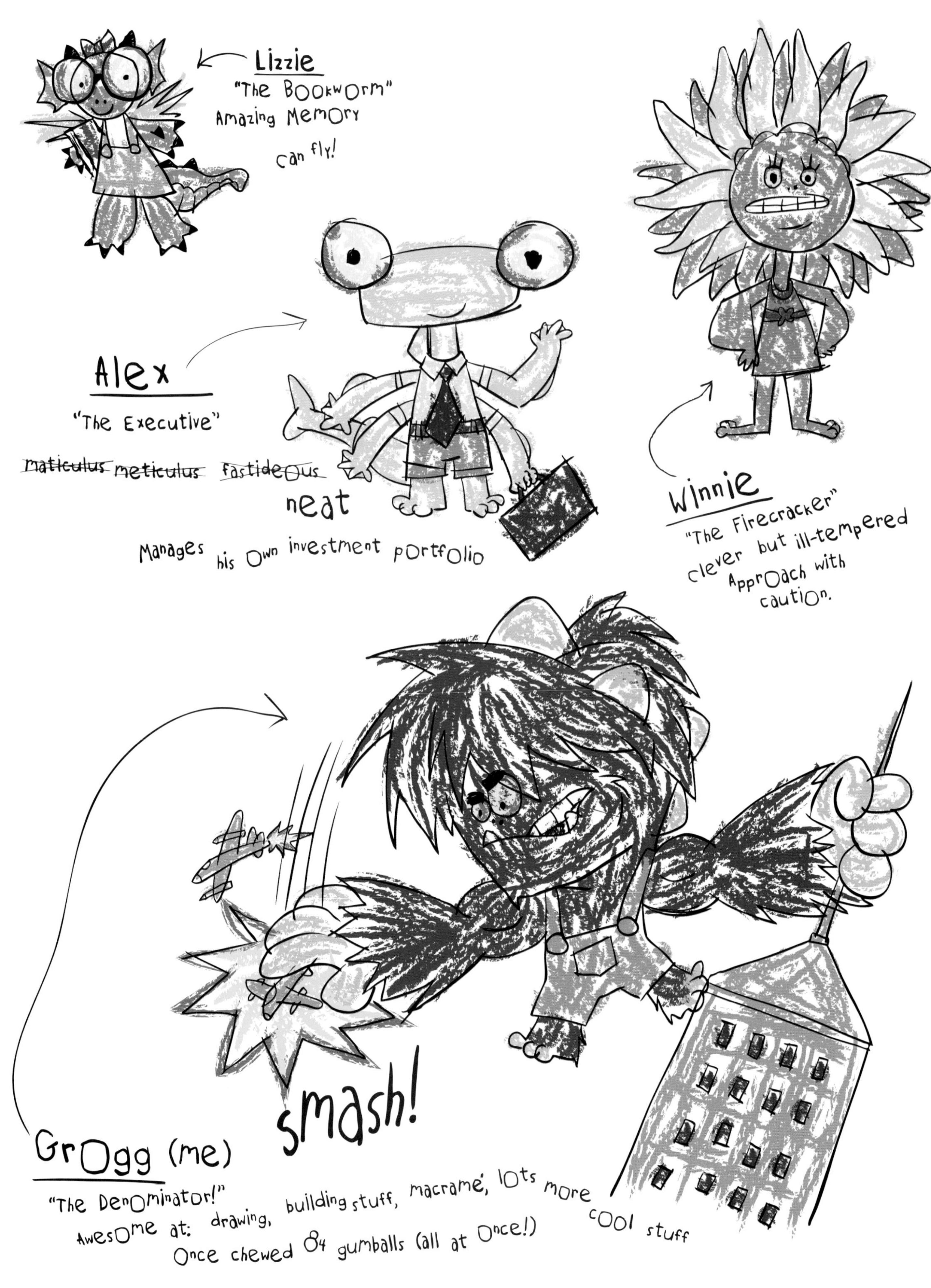
Lizzie
"The Bookworm"
Amazing Memory
can fly!
Alex
"The Executive"
~~maticulus~~ ~~meticulus~~ ~~fastideous~~
neat
Manages his own investment portfolio
Winnie
"The Firecracker"
clever but ill-tempered
Approach with caution.
smash!
Grogg (me)
"The Denominator!"
Awesome at: drawing, building stuff, macramé, lots more cool stuff
Once chewed 84 gumballs (all at once!)

Sergeant Rote
Senior Drill Instructor
(Gym Teacher)
hide and seek
champion
Professor Grok
math lab
easily abducted by
"Calamitous Clod"
Captain Kraken
shop teacher (ex-pirate)
"spins yarns" about "plunderin"
KRAK!
Mr. Wriggles
ms. Q
math teacher
always has extra supplies
faster than she looks
breathes
under water
Rosencrantz
and
Guildenstern
~~custodians~~ ~~custodian~~ custodians
hard to remember who is who
Once, when Ralph threw up in class, they put
sawdust on it.
Fiona
math team coach
knows lots of
cool tricks
soccer team captain
1

The Headmaster
How to use this book

Welcome to Beast Academy!

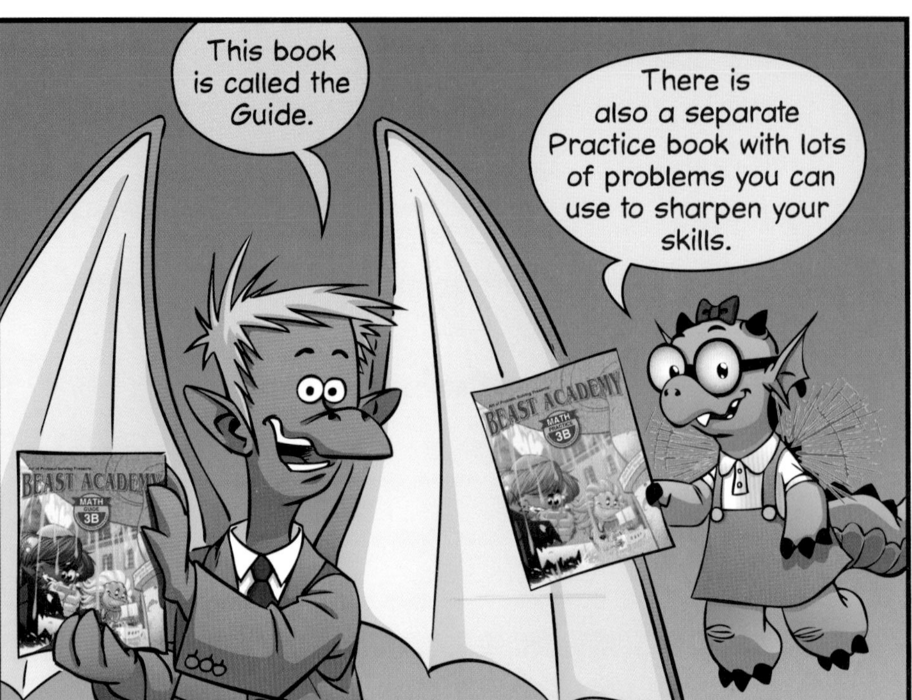
This book is called the Guide.
There is also a separate Practice book with lots of problems you can use to sharpen your skills.
BEAST ACADEMY
MATH
3B
BEAST ACADEMY
MATH
3B

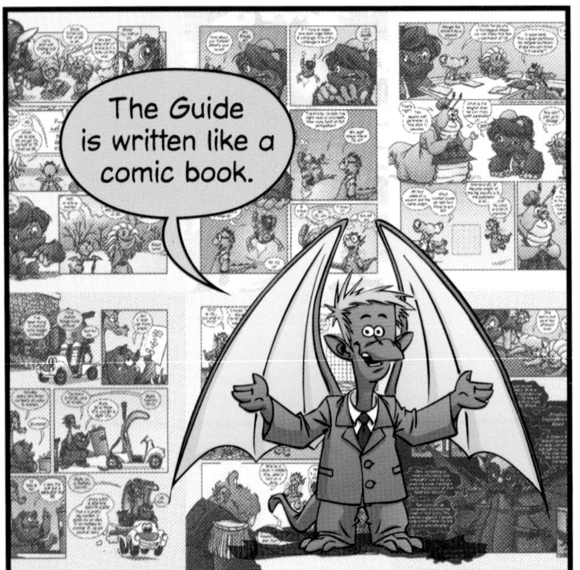
The Guide is written like a comic book.

In a comic book, whatever I say shows up in these bubbles. They're called comic balloons.
Here's one!

Each character has a different balloon color. This makes it easy to tell who is talking.
My balloons are purple!

The story is told in panels.
Panels usually have a rectangular frame around them...
...like this one.

But sometimes, panels don't have frames...
...like the open panel I'm in now.
If you've gotten this far, you probably know a little bit about how to read a comic book.
You read a comic book the same way you read any other book... from left to right and from top to bottom.
On each page, start in the top left panel.
Go to the right, then down.
Read all of the balloons in each panel from left to right and top to bottom before moving to the next panel.
At first, you may need to think about which balloon to read next.
Like when lots of characters are talking.
Right! And sometimes several balloons get connected.
Or when a character speaks more than once.
With a little practice, reading comics becomes natural.
How many panels are on this page?

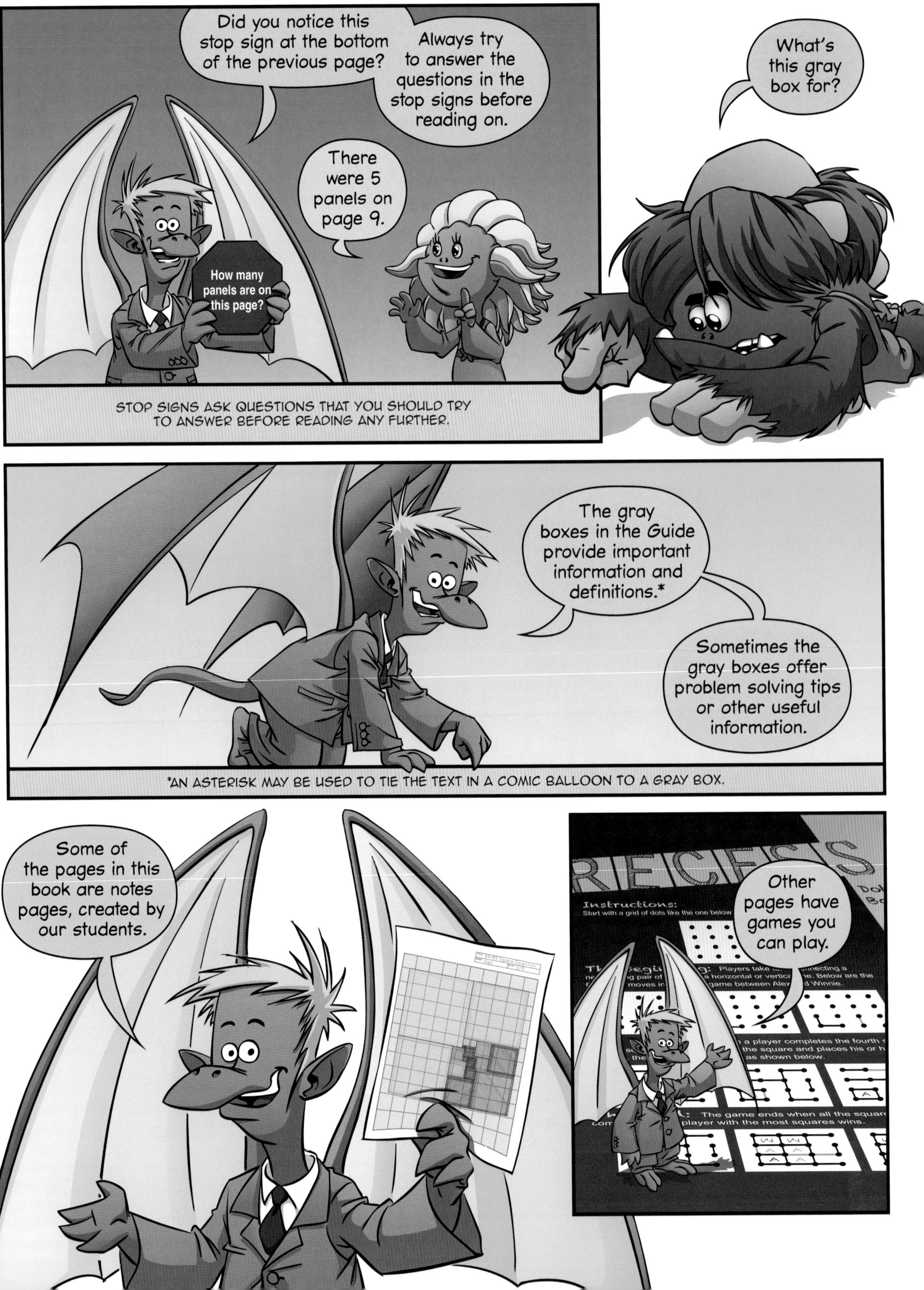

Did you notice this stop sign at the bottom of the previous page?

Always try to answer the questions in the stop signs before reading on.

What's this gray box for?

There were 5 panels on page 9.

How many panels are on this page?

STOP SIGNS ASK QUESTIONS THAT YOU SHOULD TRY TO ANSWER BEFORE READING ANY FURTHER.

The gray boxes in the Guide provide important information and definitions.*

Sometimes the gray boxes offer problem solving tips or other useful information.

*AN ASTERISK MAY BE USED TO TIE THE TEXT IN A COMIC BALLOON TO A GRAY BOX.

Some of the pages in this book are notes pages, created by our students.

Other pages have games you can play.

Practice: Pages 6, 44, and 74

Contents: Chapter 4

See page 6 in the Practice book for a recommended reading/practice sequence for Chapter 4.

Chapter 4: Multiplication

R & G
St. Ives
I heard a clever riddle today.
Does it involve an albatross sandwich?
Nope.
Then I'm interested.

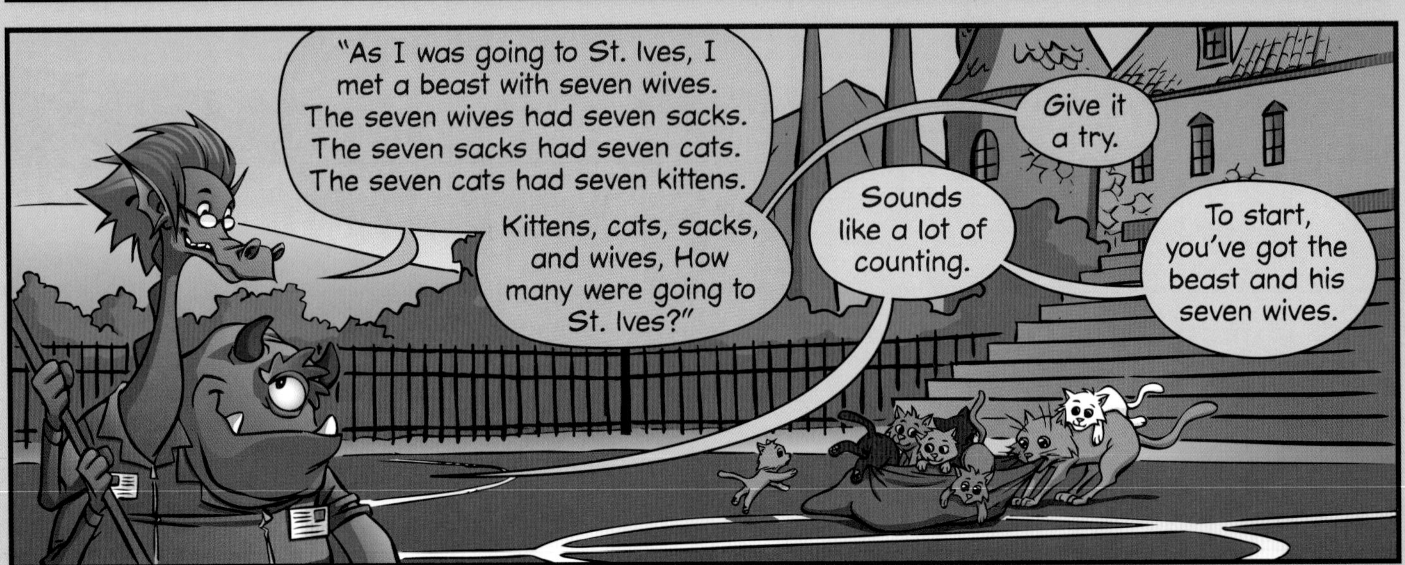
"As I was going to St. Ives, I met a beast with seven wives. The seven wives had seven sacks. The seven sacks had seven cats. The seven cats had seven kittens.
Kittens, cats, sacks, and wives, How many were going to St. Ives?"
Give it a try.
Sounds like a lot of counting.
To start, you've got the beast and his seven wives.

Go on.
Each wife had seven sacks, so we have 7+7+7+7+7+7+7 sacks. That makes...
7
14
21
28
35
42
49
sacks.

Each of the 49 sacks has 7 cats. That's a ***lot*** of skip-counting! Here goes:
7
14
21
28...

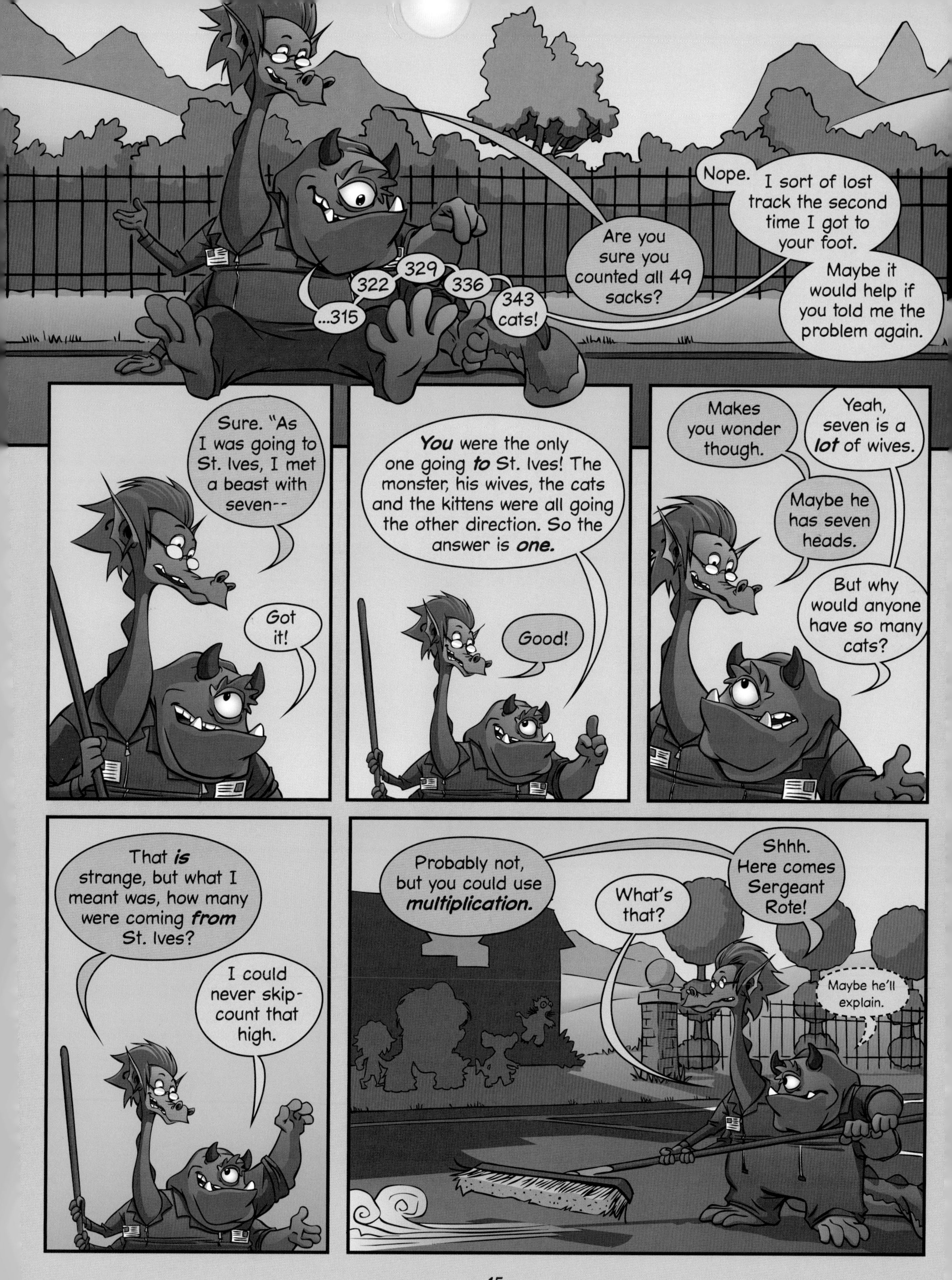

...315
322
329
336
343 cats!
Are you sure you counted all 49 sacks?
Nope.
I sort of lost track the second time I got to your foot.
Maybe it would help if you told me the problem again.

Sure. "As I was going to St. Ives, I met a beast with seven--
Got it!

You were the only one going *to* St. Ives! The monster, his wives, the cats and the kittens were all going the other direction. So the answer is *one.*
Good!

Makes you wonder though.
Yeah, seven is a *lot* of wives.
Maybe he has seven heads.
But why would anyone have so many cats?

G*Y*M
THE TIMES TABLE
I am Sergeant Rote, your Senior Drill Instructor. From now on, you will speak only when spoken to, and the first and last words out of your fangless mouths will be "Sir!" Do you understand?
Sir, yes, sir!
If you polliwogs leave this Academy, if you survive beast training, you will become masters of computation.

Until that day you are slime! You are not even fit to carry an abacus!
My orders are to weed out those who do not pack the computational capability to serve in my beloved Academy!

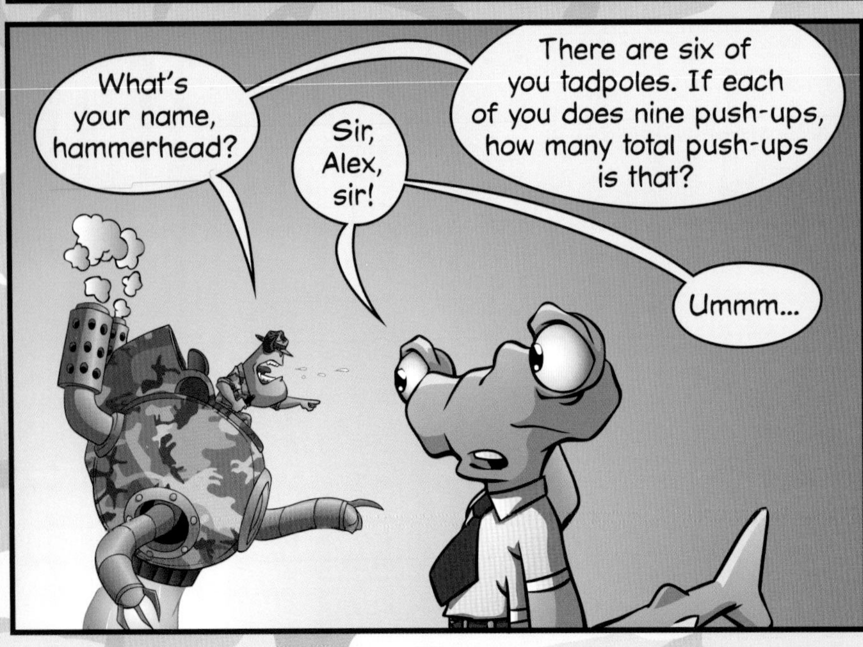
What's your name, hammerhead?
Sir, Alex, sir!
There are six of you tadpoles. If each of you does nine push-ups, how many total push-ups is that?
Ummm...

"Ummm" is not an acceptable answer! Six times nine is 54! Drop and give me 54!

How about you, furball? What's your name?
Sir, Grogg, sir!
If I have 6 cages, and each cage holds 8 octapugs, how many octapugs is that?
8, 16, 24, 32, 40, 48...
Sir, 48, sir!
Good, now drop and give me 48! There'll be no mumbling or finger-counting in this Academy!
The chomp monster has eight rows of nine teeth. How many teeth is that all together?
Sir, eight times nine is 72, sir!
Good work, tinkerbell! What's 7 times 6?
Sir, 42, sir!
8 times 4?
Sir, 32, sir!
7 times 7?
Sir, 49, sir!

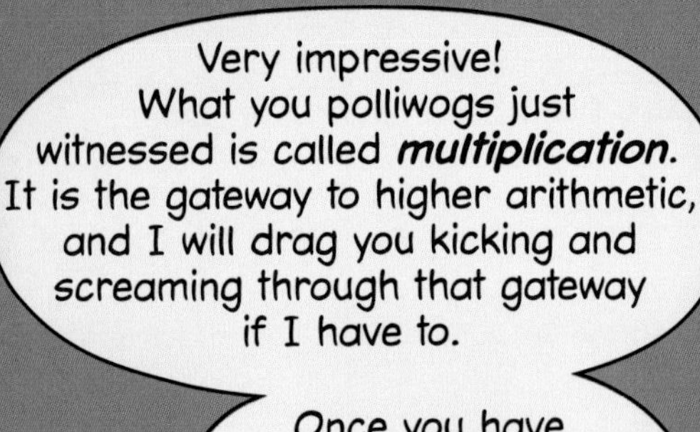
Very impressive! What you polliwogs just witnessed is called **multiplication**. It is the gateway to higher arithmetic, and I will drag you kicking and screaming through that gateway if I have to.

Once you have learned to multiply, you will no longer **add** 7 nine times, you will **multiply** 9 times 7.*

*WE WRITE "NINE TIMES SEVEN" LIKE THIS: 9×7. THE SYMBOL FOR MULTIPLICATION LOOKS LIKE THE LETTER "X" AND IS READ AS "TIMES."

Your skip-counting days are over. From now on, you will **memorize** all the facts you need to master my drills.
These facts can all be neatly organized onto one very important piece of paper.

I am handing each of you a **times table**. You must know it like you know your own claws. Repeat what is written on the back.

This is my times table. There are many like it, but this one is mine. My times table, without me, is useless. Without my times table, I am useless. I must master each of its rows and each of its columns until it has become a part of me. I will.
Very good. **Dismissed!**

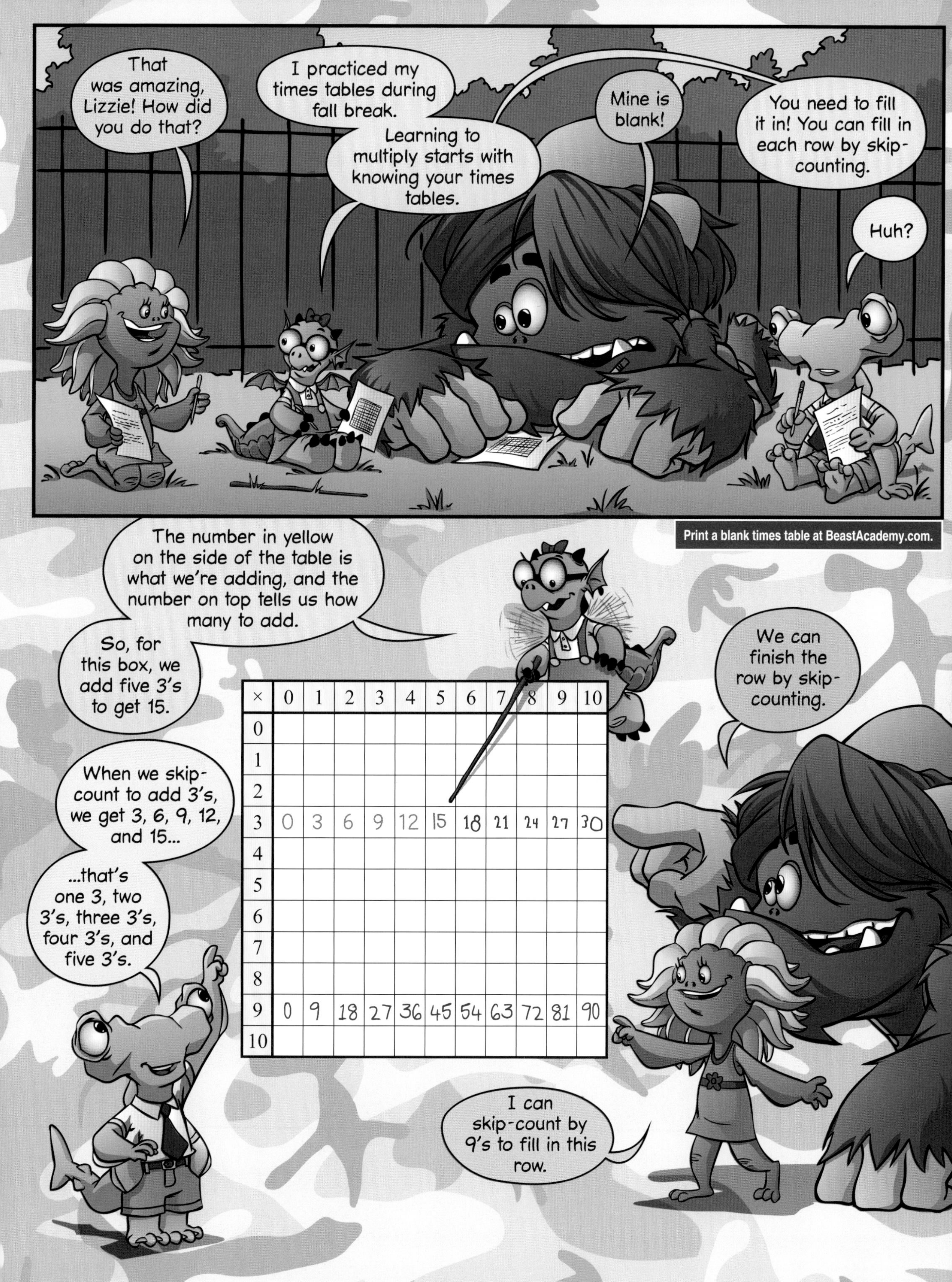

×	0	1	2	3	4	5	6	7	8	9	10
0											
1											
2											
3	0	3	6	9	12	15	18	21	24	27	30
4											
5											
6											
7											
8											
9	0	9	18	27	36	45	54	63	72	81	90
10											

×	0	1	2	3	4	5	6	7	8	9	10
0											
1											
2											
3	0	3	6	9	12	15	18	21	24	27	3
4	0	4	8	12	16	20	24	28	32	36	4
5											
6	0	6	12	18	24	30	36	42	48	54	60
7	0	7	14	21	28	35	42	49	56	63	70
8											
9	0	9	18	27	36	45	54	63	72	81	90
10											

×	0	1	2	3	4	5	6	7	8	9	10
0	0	0	0	0	0	0	0	0	0	0	0
1	0	1	2	3	4	5	6	7	8	9	10
2	0	2	4	6	8	10	12	14	16	18	20
3	0	3	6	9	12	15	18	21	24	27	30
4	0	4	8	12	16	20	24	28	32	36	40
5	0	5	10	15	20	25	30	35	40	45	50
6	0	6	12	18	24	30	36	42	48	54	60
7	0	7	14	21	28	35	42	49	56	63	70
8	0	8	16	24	32	40	48	56	64	72	80
9	0	9	18	27	36	45	54	63	72	81	90
10	0	10	20	30	40	50	60	70	80	90	100

If you want to add six 7's... that is the same thing as multiplying "6 times 7." You can see from the table that 6 times 7 is 42.
What if you don't have your table?
You have to ***know*** all the answers.
Ugh! We have to memorize all of the answers on the table?!?
Not really. You ***already*** know most of them.
Like the ones!
Right, You don't really need to memorize ***those***, because adding one of any number is that number.
One seven is 7!
And adding any number of ones gives you that number.
Five ones is 5!
What other easy rows and columns can you find?

×	0	1	2	3	4	5	6	7	8	9	10
0	0	0	0	0	0	0	0	0	0	0	0
1	0	1	2	3	4	5	6	7	8	9	10
2	0	2	4	6	8	10	12	14	16	18	20
3	0	3	6	9	12	15	18	21	24	27	30
4	0	4	8	12	16	20	24	28	32	36	40
5	0	5	10	15	20	25	30	35	40	45	50
6	0	6	12	18	24	30	36	42	48	54	60
7	0	7	14	21	28	35	42	49	56	63	70
8	0	8	16	24	32	40	48	56	64	72	80
9	0	9	18	27	36	45	54	63	72	81	90
10	0	10	20	30	40	50	60	70	80	90	100

×	0	1	2	3	4	5	6	7	8	9	10
0	0	0	0	0	0	0	0	0	0	0	0
1	0	1	2	3	4	5	6	7	8	9	10
2	0	2	4	6	8	10	12	14	16	18	20
3	0	3	6	9	12	15	18	21	24	27	30
4	0	4	8	12	16	20	24	28	32	36	40
5	0	5	10	15	20	25	30	35	40	45	50
6	0	6	12	18	24	30	36	42	48	54	60
7	0	7	14	21	28	35	42	49	56	63	70
8	0	8	16	24	32	40	48	56	64	72	80
9	0	9	18	27	36	45	54	63	72	81	90
10	0	10	20	30	40	50	60	70	80	90	100

×	0	1	2	3	4	5	6	7	8	9	10
0	0	0	0	0	0	0	0	0	0	0	0
1	0	1	2	3	4	5	6	7	8	9	10
2	0	2	4	6	8	10	12	14	16	18	20
3	0	3	6	9	12	15	18	21	24	27	30
4	0	4	8	12	16	20	24	28	32	36	40
5	0	5	10	15	20	25	30	35	40	45	50
6	0	6	12	18	24	30	36	42	48	54	60
7	0	7	14	21	28	35	42	49	56	63	70
8	0	8	16	24	32	40	48	56	64	72	80
9	0	9	18	27	36	45	54	63	72	81	90
10	0	10	20	30	40	50	60	70	80	90	100

There are a bunch we already know, but we still have a lot to memorize.

You still haven't found the best trick! Most of the answers on the times table have a twin.

A twin?

Can you find twins in the times table?

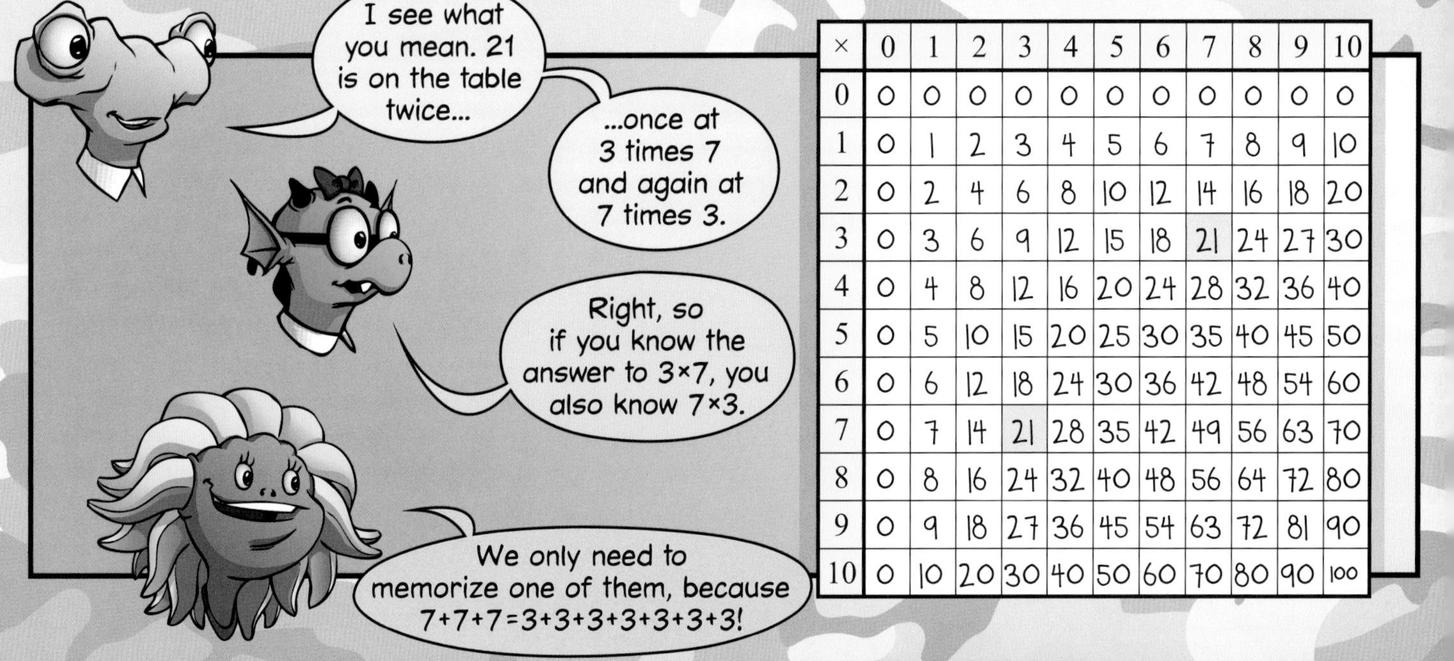

I see what you mean. 21 is on the table twice...

...once at 3 times 7 and again at 7 times 3.

Right, so if you know the answer to 3×7, you also know 7×3.

We only need to memorize one of them, because 7+7+7=3+3+3+3+3+3+3!

×	0	1	2	3	4	5	6	7	8	9	10
0	0	0	0	0	0	0	0	0	0	0	0
1	0	1	2	3	4	5	6	7	8	9	10
2	0	2	4	6	8	10	12	14	16	18	20
3	0	3	6	9	12	15	18	21	24	27	30
4	0	4	8	12	16	20	24	28	32	36	40
5	0	5	10	15	20	25	30	35	40	45	50
6	0	6	12	18	24	30	36	42	48	54	60
7	0	7	14	21	28	35	42	49	56	63	70
8	0	8	16	24	32	40	48	56	64	72	80
9	0	9	18	27	36	45	54	63	72	81	90
10	0	10	20	30	40	50	60	70	80	90	100

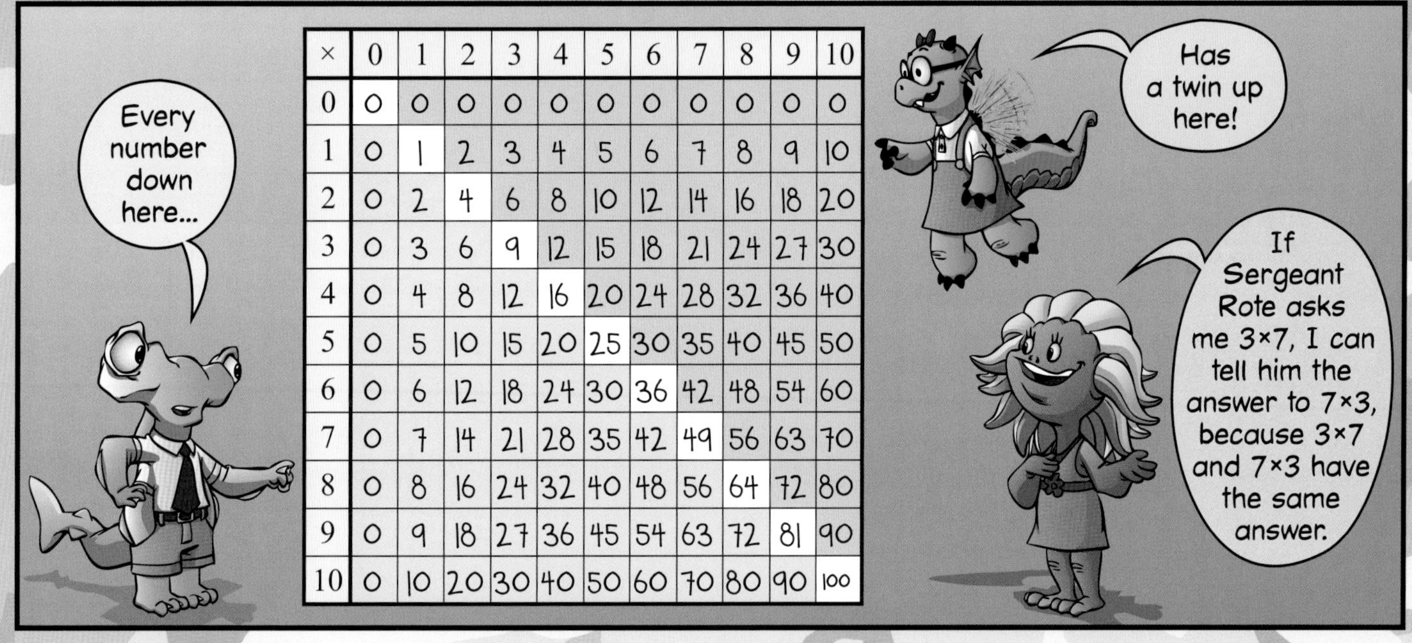

×	0	1	2	3	4	5	6	7	8	9	10
0	0	0	0	0	0	0	0	0	0	0	0
1	0	1	2	3	4	5	6	7	8	9	10
2	0	2	4	6	8	10	12	14	16	18	20
3	0	3	6	9	12	15	18	21	24	27	30
4	0	4	8	12	16	20	24	28	32	36	40
5	0	5	10	15	20	25	30	35	40	45	50
6	0	6	12	18	24	30	36	42	48	54	60
7	0	7	14	21	28	35	42	49	56	63	70
8	0	8	16	24	32	40	48	56	64	72	80
9	0	9	18	27	36	45	54	63	72	81	90
10	0	10	20	30	40	50	60	70	80	90	100

Every number down here...
Has a twin up here!
If Sergeant Rote asks me 3×7, I can tell him the answer to 7×3, because 3×7 and 7×3 have the same answer.

The numbers on the diagonal are really important to memorize. They are the entries where you multiply a number by itself.
Like 6×6!
Right. They're called ***perfect squares***.
THE NEXT CHAPTER IS ALL ABOUT PERFECT SQUARES!

Why are perfect squares important?
If you know all of the perfect squares, you can figure out a lot of the hardest multiplication problems.
What do you mean?
If you memorize 7×7=49, then 7×8 is just 7 more.
7×7 is 49, so 7×8 is 49+7=56.
You can do that with other problems too! If you know 7×8=56, then you can quickly add 7 more to get 7×9.
7×9 is 7×8 plus ***another*** 7.
7×9 =7×8+7 =56+7 =63!

×	0	1	2	3	4	5	6	7	8	9	10
0	0	0	0	0	0	0	0	0	0	0	0
1	0	1	2	3	4	5	6	7	8	9	10
2	0	2	4	6	8	10	12	14	16	18	20
3	0	3	6	9	12	15	18	21	24	27	30
4	0	4	8	12	16	20	24	28	32	36	40
5	0	5	10	15	20	25	30	35	40	45	50
6	0	6	12	18	24	30	36	42	48	54	60
7	0	7	14	21	28	35	42	49	56	63	70
8	0	8	16	24	32	40	48	56	64	72	80
9	0	9	18	27	36	45	54	63	72	81	90
10	0	10	20	30	40	50	60	70	80	90	100

×	0	1	2	3	4	5	6	7	8	9	10
0	0	0	0	0	0	0	0	0	0	0	0
1	0	1	2	3	4	5	6	7	8	9	10
2	0	2	4	6	8	10	12	14	16	18	20
3	0	3	6	9	12	15	18	21	24	27	30
4	0	4	8	12	16	20	24	28	32	36	40
5	0	5	10	15	20	25	30	35	40	45	50
6	0	6	12	18	24	30	36	42	48	54	60
7	0	7	14	21	28	35	42	49	56	63	70
8	0	8	16	24	32	40	48	56	64	72	80
9	0	9	18	27	36	45	54	63	72	81	90
10	0	10	20	30	40	50	60	70	80	90	100

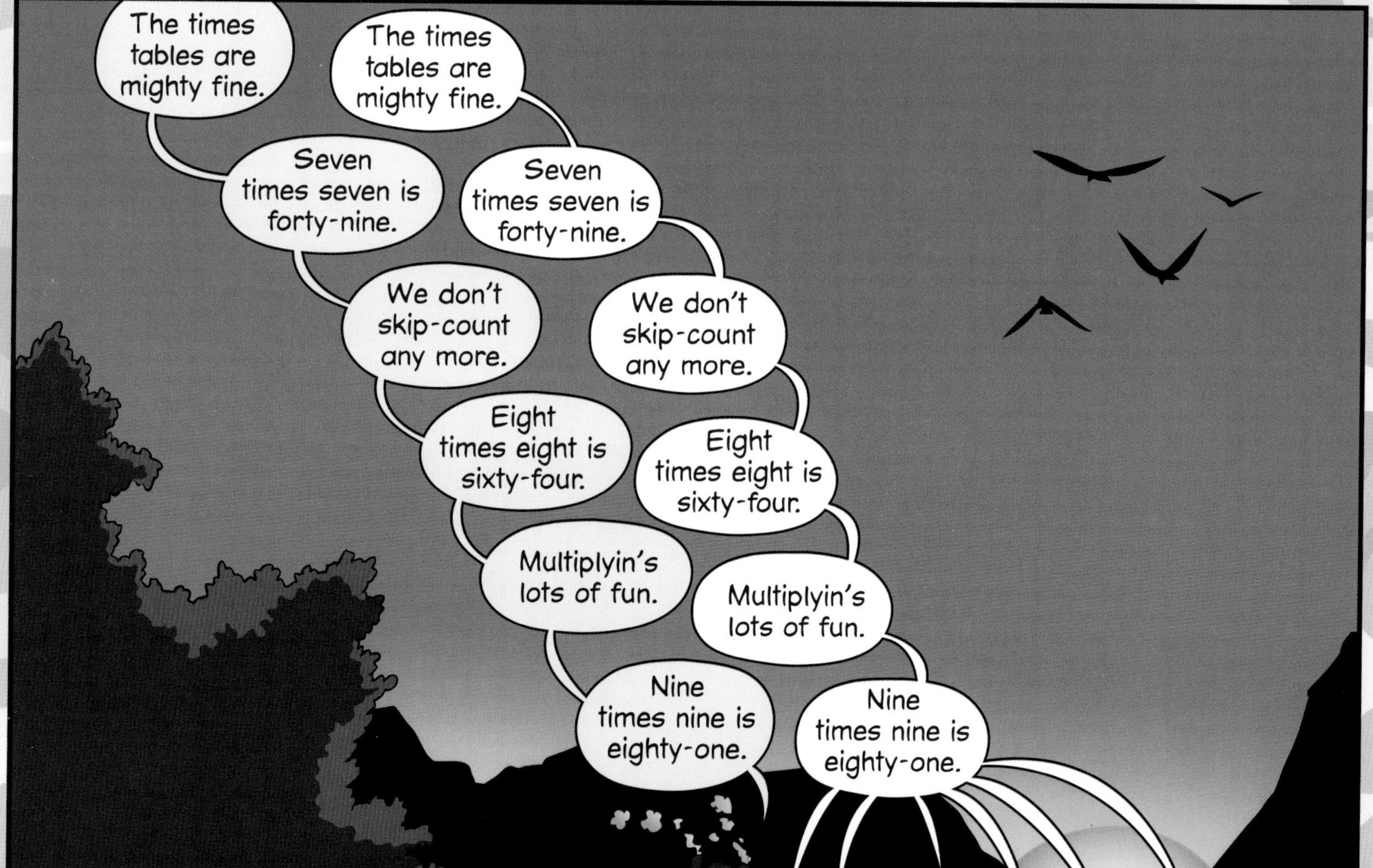

The times tables are mighty fine.

The times tables are mighty fine.

Seven times seven is forty-nine.

Seven times seven is forty-nine.

We don't skip-count any more.

We don't skip-count any more.

Eight times eight is sixty-four.

Eight times eight is sixty-four.

Multiplyin's lots of fun.

Multiplyin's lots of fun.

Nine times nine is eighty-one.

Nine times nine is eighty-one.

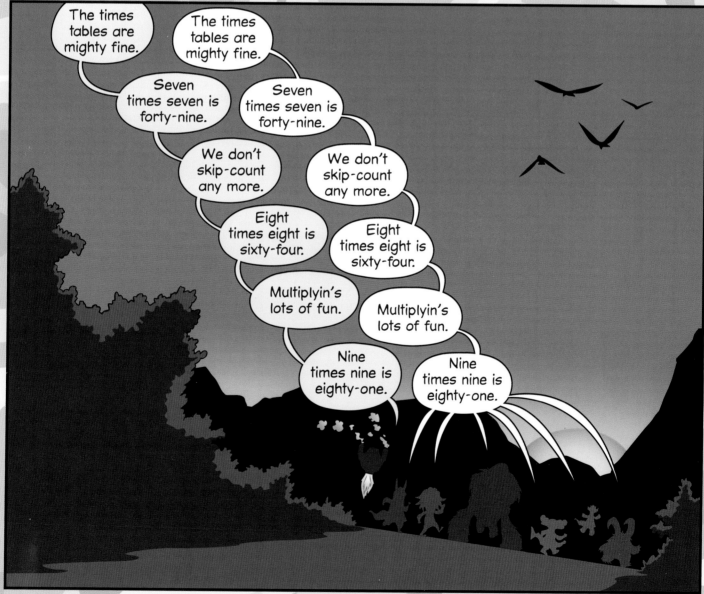

Practice: Pages 7-15

R&G
The Commutative Property
I see you've made a times table.
Want me to help you practice?
I got pretty tired of skip-counting and decided to give this multiplication stuff a try.
Sure. Quiz me.
Termites
TRASH SORTING

2×6?
12.
6×7?
42.
6×6?
36.
6×8?
48.
9×6?
54.
You got all five!
Those were sixes.
I only asked you five.
There weren't any fives at all, they were all sixes. Ask me some sevens.
You want seven?
As many as you want, just make sure to include some sevens.
Ahhh, *sevens!*

Try these:
7×5?
35.
7×2?
14.
4×7?
28.
5×7?
You already asked that one.
I asked you 7×5.
But it's the same thing!
Is it?

It's easy to explain after you've learned about area.
To find the area of a rectangle, we can just multiply its height by its width.

Sure. A rectangle that is three squares high and five squares wide has 3×5=15 squares.

Turning the rectangle over on its side doesn't change its area.
I guess not.
3+3+3+3+3=5+5+5.
5×3=3×5.

So, when you multiply two numbers, order doesn't matter.*
That's right.

*THIS IS THE ***COMMUTATIVE PROPERTY OF MULTIPLICATION***. WHEN WE MULTIPLY TWO NUMBERS, WE CAN MULTIPLY THE FIRST NUMBER BY THE SECOND, OR THE SECOND NUMBER BY THE FIRST.

BLOCK BLOB

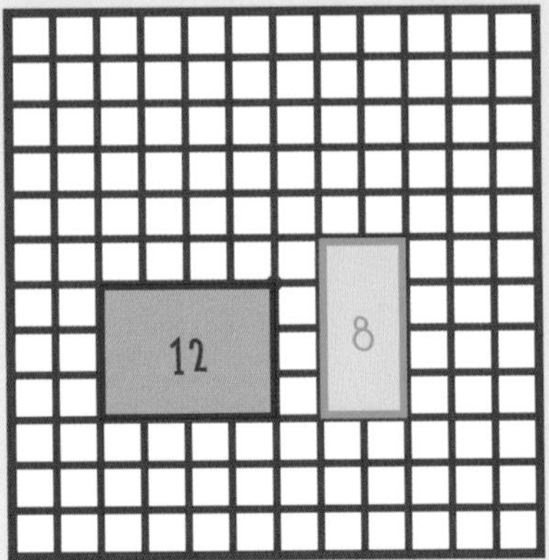

The Beginning: Grogg and Lizzie are playing a game of Block Blob. Grogg rolls a pair of standard dice. The numbers Grogg rolls give him the length and width of a rectangle which he must trace on the 12×12 game board. Grogg's first rectangle must have one of its corners on the dot at the center of the board. Grogg writes the area of his rectangle inside of it. His rectangle is shown in purple.

Lizzie rolls next and uses a different color to trace her rectangle anywhere on the game board, but not overlapping Grogg's rectangle. Lizzie writes the area of her rectangle. Her rectangle is shown in green.

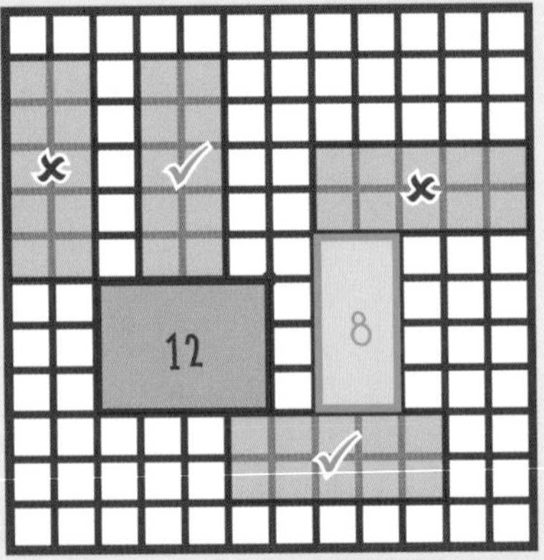

The Middle: Grogg and Lizzie continue taking turns rolling the dice and tracing new rectangles on the board. When a player traces a new rectangle, it must touch a side (not just a corner) of any rectangle that he or she has already drawn. The attached purple rectangles form Grogg's Block Blob. The green ones form Lizzie's Block Blob.

For example, if Grogg rolls a 2 and a 5 on his second roll, he can place his rectangle as marked with the green ✓'s, but not as marked with the red ✗'s.

The End: When a player rolls a rectangle that cannot be placed on the board, he or she must pass. The game ends when there are four passes in a row (two for each player).

When the game ends, each player adds the areas of all the rectangles in his or her Block Blob. The player whose Block Blob has the largest area wins.

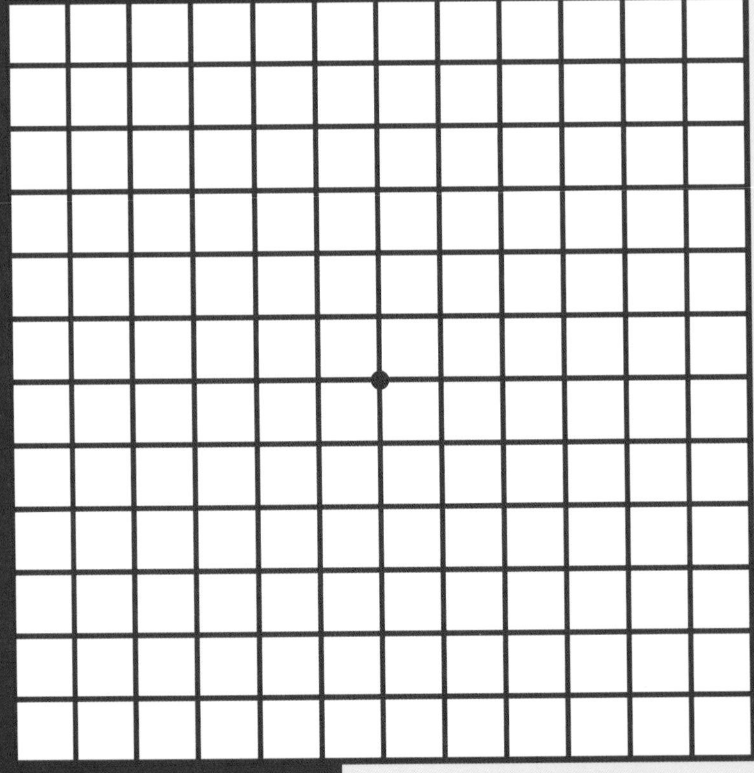

Print as many game boards as you want at BeastAcademy.com

I've been trying to multiply some bigger numbers.
That makes things more difficult.
Not for me...

...but it does use more paper.
8×6=48

Actually, some very large numbers are easy to multiply.
Example?

You know 3×10=30, and 8×10=80.
Sure, 30 is three 10's, and 80 is eight 10's.
Right. Now try 13×10.

13 tens is 130.
I see. You just put a ***zero*** after the ***13!***

Right, so to multiply 222×10...
...since 2,220 is 222 tens, 222×10=2,220!
Uh huh...
That ***is*** a pretty big number. It gives me an idea. If we multiply by another 10, we get another zero.

Well, 34×10×10 is the same as 34×100...
That's thirty-four hundred! We get *two* zeros after the 34!
Right, and 34×1,000 is 34,000.
Of course, thirty-four thousand.

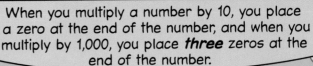

When you multiply a number by 10, you place a zero at the end of the number, and when you multiply by 1,000, you place *three* zeros at the end of the number.
And when you multiply a number by 1,000,000,000,000 you would place 12 zeros!
MIND THE LEDGE

It's the same as multiplying by 10 a bunch of times.
12 times in a row!

I wonder... ...if we multiply 9×10, we get 90. What about 9×20?

Since 20 is two tens, 9×20 is just 9 times two tens...
...9×2×10!

That gives us 18×10.
And 18×10 is 180!

So to multiply 9×20, you just multiply the 9 by the 2 and put a zero at the end.
So 7×80 is 560...
...I just did 7×8 and put on a zero.

5×90 is 450!
70×4 is 280!
20×6 is 120!
90×3 is 270!

Hmmm... What about 90×30?
If 90×3 is 270, then 90×30 just needs another zero.

90×30 is 2,700.
It's 9×3 with *two* zeros at the end!
Right, because 90×30 is just 90×3...
...times 10!
XING

And 90×300 has one more zero.
27,000!

And 900,000 times 30,000,000,000?
900,000 has five zeros, and 30,000,000,000 has ten, so we get a 27 with 5+10=*15* zeros on the end... 27,000,000,000,000,000!

Practice: Pages 16-29

Ms. Q.
The Associative Property
Did everyone bring graph paper?
I forgot mine at home, Ms. Q.
I can share. I have quad-ruled, engineering, and isometric.
What does everyone need?

How nice, Alex!
Each student needs four sheets of quad-ruled paper.
How many sheets is that all together?

There are two tables...
...five of us at each table...
...and we each need four sheets.

Two tables times five monsters makes 10 monsters...
...and 10 monsters times 4 sheets each makes 10×4=40 sheets of graph paper.
I did it differently, but I got the same answer.
Each table has five monsters. Each monster gets four sheets of paper. That's 5×4=20 sheets per table. With two tables, that's 20×2=40 sheets.

It's the same multiplication problem solved two different ways.
What do you mean, Alex?

Winnie and Lizzie both multiplied 2×5×4.

Winnie did 2×5 first, then multiplied by 4.

Lizzie did 5×4 first, then multiplied by 2.

Winnie	Lizzie
(2×5)×4	2×(5×4)
10×4	2×20
40	40

PARENTHESES LET YOU KNOW WHAT TO DO FIRST. IF PART OF A PROBLEM IS WRITTEN INSIDE PARENTHESES, YOU SHOULD START THE PROBLEM BY SOLVING WHAT IS INSIDE THE PARENTHESES.

((2×3)×5)×6   2×(3×(5×6))   (2×(3×5))×6   2×((3×5)×6)   (2×3)×(5×6)

When you multiply three numbers, you can start by multiplying the first two ***or*** by multiplying the last two.

Good, Lizzie!

How can we multiply more than three numbers?

Does the ***product*** of four numbers change when the parentheses change?

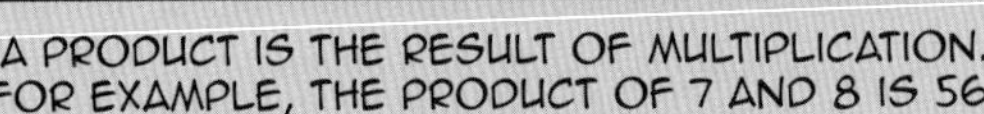

A PRODUCT IS THE RESULT OF MULTIPLICATION. FOR EXAMPLE, THE PRODUCT OF 7 AND 8 IS 56.

Try them all.

((2×3)×5)×6	2×(3×(5×6))	(2×(3×5))×6	2×((3×5)×6)	(2×3)×(5×6)
(6×5)×6	2×(3×30)	(2×15)×6	2×(15×6)	6 × 30
30×6	2×90	30×6	2×90	180
180	180 (by Winnie)	180	180	

15 + 15 = 30; 15 + 15 = 30; 15 + 15 = 30; 90

Changing the parentheses didn't change the answer.

We all got the same thing!

When you multiply a bunch of numbers, you can put parentheses wherever you want.*

But why do we need more than one way to multiply numbers?

*THIS IS CALLED THE *ASSOCIATIVE PROPERTY OF MULTIPLICATION*.

Try this. How would you multiply 9×2×5?
9×2 is 18, and 18×5 is...
...ummm...
To solve 9×2×5, you ***could*** multiply 2×5 first...
...9×2×5 is 9×(2×5), which is 9×10.
90!
It's easier to multiply the 2×5 first because 2×5=10.
To multiply a number by ten, you just put a zero at the end.
2×7×5×3
That's right!
How could you make this problem easier to solve?
We want to get the 2 and the 5 together.
We can rearrange the numbers like this...
...and group them like this!
2×7×5×3
2×5×7×3
(2×5)×(7×3)
10×21
210
10×21 is 210!

We can multiply as many numbers as we want in any order we want!
THAT'S RIGHT! WE CAN MULTIPLY AS MANY NUMBERS AS WE WANT IN ANY ORDER WE WANT.

So if we want to multiply 5×5×9×3×2×2...
...we can pair the fives with twos.
It makes the multiplication easier.
5×5×9×3×2×2 = (9×3)×(2×5)×(2×5)
= 27 × 10 × 10
= 2700

When we want to multiply a bunch of numbers, the commutative property lets us change the order of the numbers.
The associative property lets us put parentheses wherever we want.

My dad ***commutes*** to work with his ***associates.***
?!?

He commutes. That means he switches places, from home to work.
Like how numbers switch places when you use the commutative property!

His associates are his group of friends.
Like the groups you make with the associative property!
You guys are so lame.

MATH TEAM
...with Fiona!
Today we're going to learn a few tricks that will help you keep up with the Bots.
First, you need to get really good at doubling numbers.
43 +43 86 21 +21 42
Doubling a number just means you add it to itself.
Some numbers are really easy to double, like 43 and 21. You just double both digits.
But numbers with bigger digits like 27 or 76 are a lot harder to double in your head.
43 +43 86 21 +21 42 27 +27 54
Here's the trick...
...think of the tens digit and the ones digit separately.
I get it!
27 is 20 plus 7. To double 27, we can double 20 and 7 separately and then add the results.
Two 20's equal 40, and two 7's equal 14, so 27+27 is 40+14=54.
76+76 is two 70's plus two 6's. That makes 140+12=152!
That *is* easier!

Can you find an easy way to multiply by 8?

Let's start with finding half of 60.
Since 30+30=60, half of 60 is 30.
You just take half of 6 and put a zero on the end.
Good! Try half of 70.
Hmmm... What number can we double to get 70?
35!
When we double 35, we get 70, so half of 70 must be 35.
Excellent! Try a few more:
Find half of:
50
640
430
Try them!
Since 25¢+25¢=50¢, it's easy to remember that half of 50 is 25.
Half of 640 is 320! Since 32+32=64, 320+320=640.
Half of 430 is harder.
Half of 430 is just half of 400 plus half of 30.
Half of 400 is 200, and half of 30 is 15. 200+15=215!
Great work!

This next trick gives us an easy way to multiply large numbers by 5.
Try this.
Take a number, multiply it by ten, then find half of the result.
9×10 is 90, and half of 90 is 45.
It's the same as 9 times 5.
Multiplying by 10 then finding half is the same as multiplying by five!
10
5
5
9
=
+
Why does ***that*** work?
9×10 is the same as 9×5 plus 9×5...
...so half of 9×10 is 9×5!
5
5
9
To multiply by 5, we can multiply by 10 and take half!
That's right. Try a few more.
26×5= 62×5= 47×5= 54×5=
Try to solve all four of these in your head.

26×10 is 260, and half of 260 is 130...
SKRATCH SKRATCH
...so 26×5 is 130!
62×5 is just half of 620...
...310!
47×5 is just half of 470, which is half of 400 plus half of 70...
...200+35= 235!
54×5 is half of 540...
...that's half of 500 plus half of 40...
...250+20= 270!
Try 85×5.
85... 850...
425!
44×5
44... 440...
220!
23×5
23... 230...
115!
2,648×5.
13,240!
Hey, no fair!
Whoa!
You guys are good.

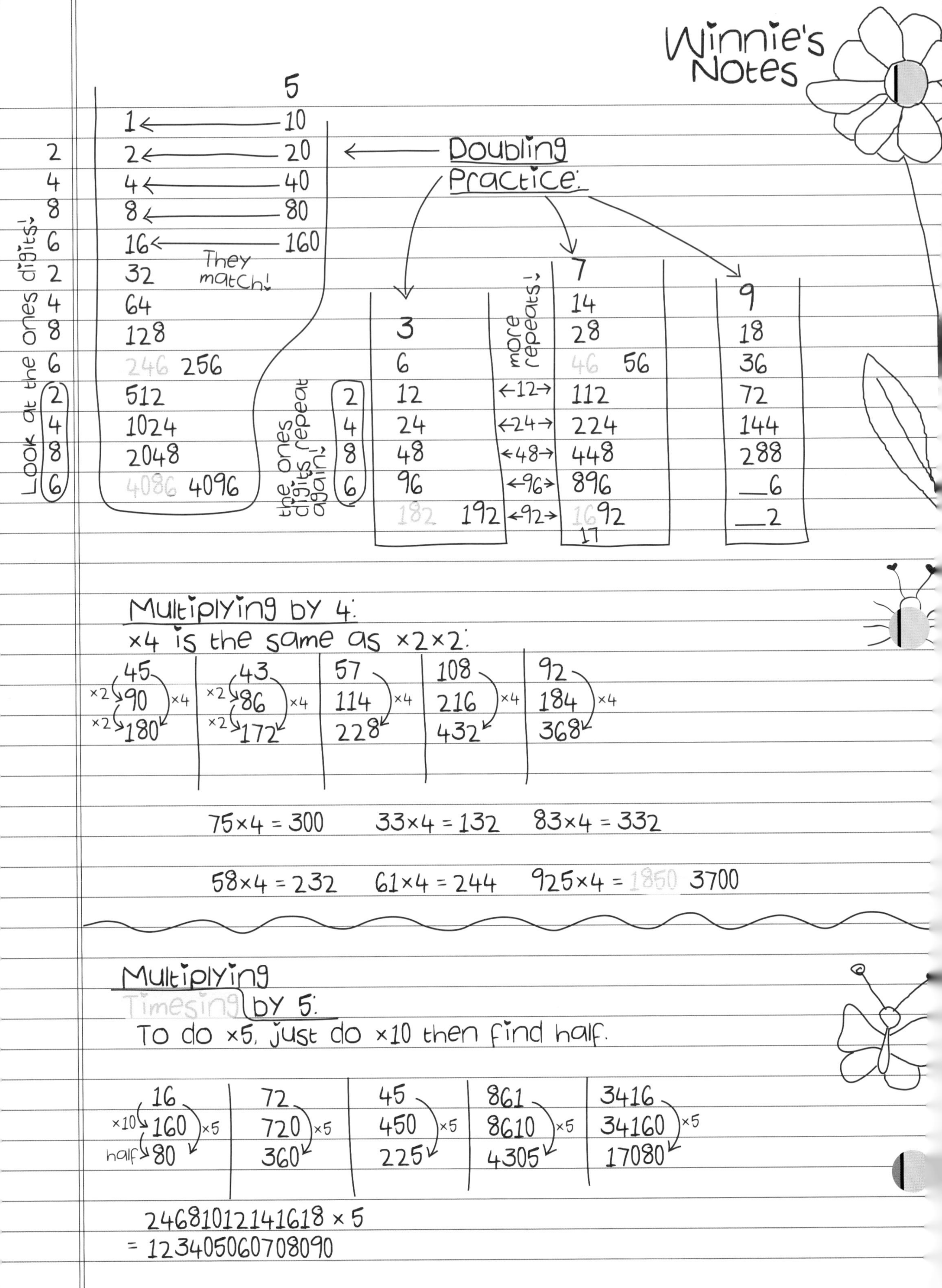

Winnie's Notes
5
1 2 4 8 16 32 64 128 256 512 1024 2048 4096
10 20 40 80 160
They match!
Look at the ones digits! 2 4 8 6 2 4 8 6 2 4 8 6
Doubling Practice:
3
6 12 24 48 96 192
the ones digits repeat again! 2 4 8 6
more repeats!
7
14 28 56 112 224 448 896 1692
←12→ ←24→ ←48→ ←96→ ←92→
9
18 36 72 144 288 __6 __2
Multiplying by 4:
×4 is the same as ×2×2:
45 ×2 90 ×2 180 ×4
43 ×2 86 ×2 172 ×4
57 114 228 ×4
108 216 432 ×4
92 184 368 ×4
75×4 = 300
33×4 = 132
83×4 = 332
58×4 = 232
61×4 = 244
925×4 = 3700
Multiplying by 5:
To do ×5, just do ×10 then find half.
16 ×10 160 half 80 ×5
72 720 360 ×5
45 450 225 ×5
861 8610 4305 ×5
3416 34160 17080 ×5
24681012141618 × 5
= 12340506070809O

THE LAB
PENNY ROWS
Multiplication is a splendid shortcut for counting lots of objects if they are organized.
For example, I brought 6 cups of 9 pennies to class today. If I asked you how many pennies there are, you wouldn't want to dump them all out to count them.
You could just multiply 6 times 9 to get 54.
Do we get to keep these?
If I asked you to count the number of squares on a chess board, you wouldn't count them one at a time.
The board is 8 squares wide and 8 squares tall, so it has 8×8=64 squares.
Qh4? You sank my Scrabbleship!
But for today's lesson, it might just help to forget about multiplication.
Done!
Your first task is to make two rows of five pennies. How many pennies will you need?
10!
9!
ugh
You *can* do it with just 9!
Can you find a way to make 2 rows of 5 pennies using only 9 pennies?

Bwah Ha Ha! Professor Grok is gone. I've abducted your educator. It's time for something much more diabolically difficult...

...Practically Impossible Penny Rows!

It doesn't ta brilliant beast to create a clever coin composition with just *two* rows. Making more rows can myst the most mast monsters

Only completing a most confounding coin composition can help you crack the code, creating a clue for the location of your illustrious educator.

Ten coins can be composed to create five rows of four coins. The solution suggests a simple symbol that marks the site of your schoolteacher.

hink fast, ecause...

...Endangerment is Imminent!!!

What did he just say?

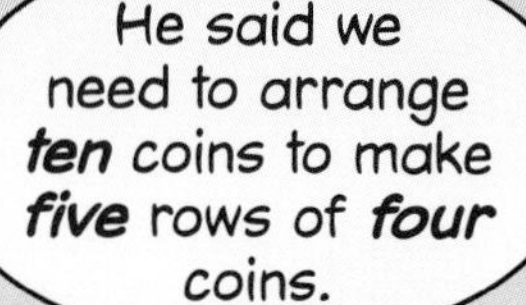
He said we need to arrange ***ten*** coins to make ***five*** rows of ***four*** coins.

Five rows of four coins! That should take 20 coins, not 10!

But some of the coins can be part of two rows.

When two rows cross, the penny where they cross is part of both rows.
Maybe we should start with something easier... like three rows of four coins.*

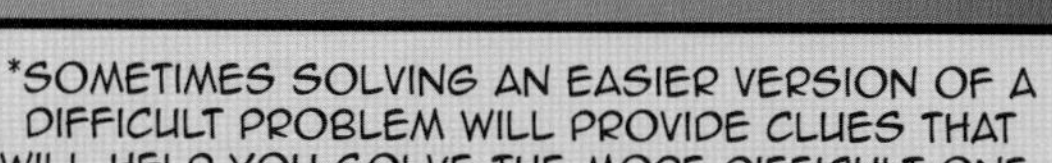
*SOMETIMES SOLVING AN EASIER VERSION OF A DIFFICULT PROBLEM WILL PROVIDE CLUES THAT WILL HELP YOU SOLVE THE MORE DIFFICULT ONE.

Got it!
I see. If we place the coins in a triangle, it only takes 9 coins to get three rows of four coins.

Three of the coins are part of two rows.
It seems like three rows of four coins would take 3×4=12 coins, but ***three*** coins were counted twice, so we only needed 12-3=9 coins!
Five rows of four coins seems like it would take 5×4=20 coins...
...but if each of the 10 coins is a part of two rows...
...then they will ***all*** get counted twice.
Can you make five rows of four coins with just 10 coins?

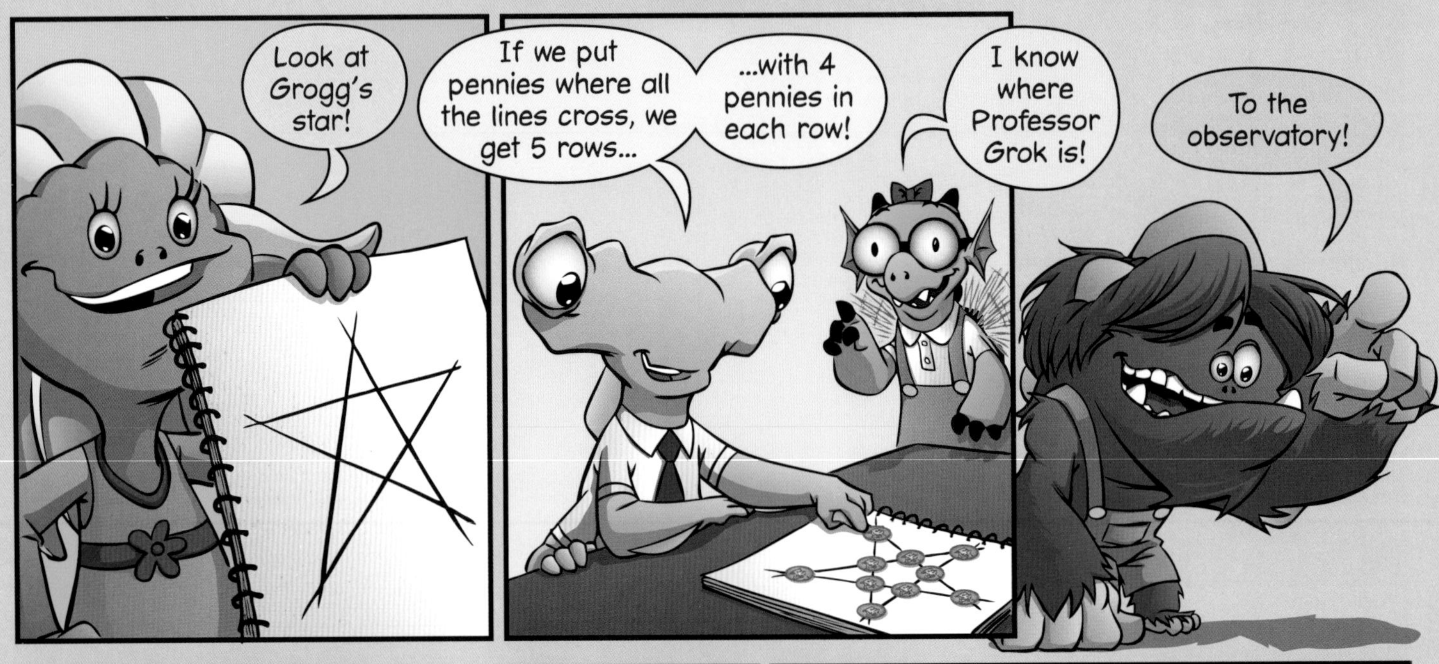

Practice: Pages 30-43

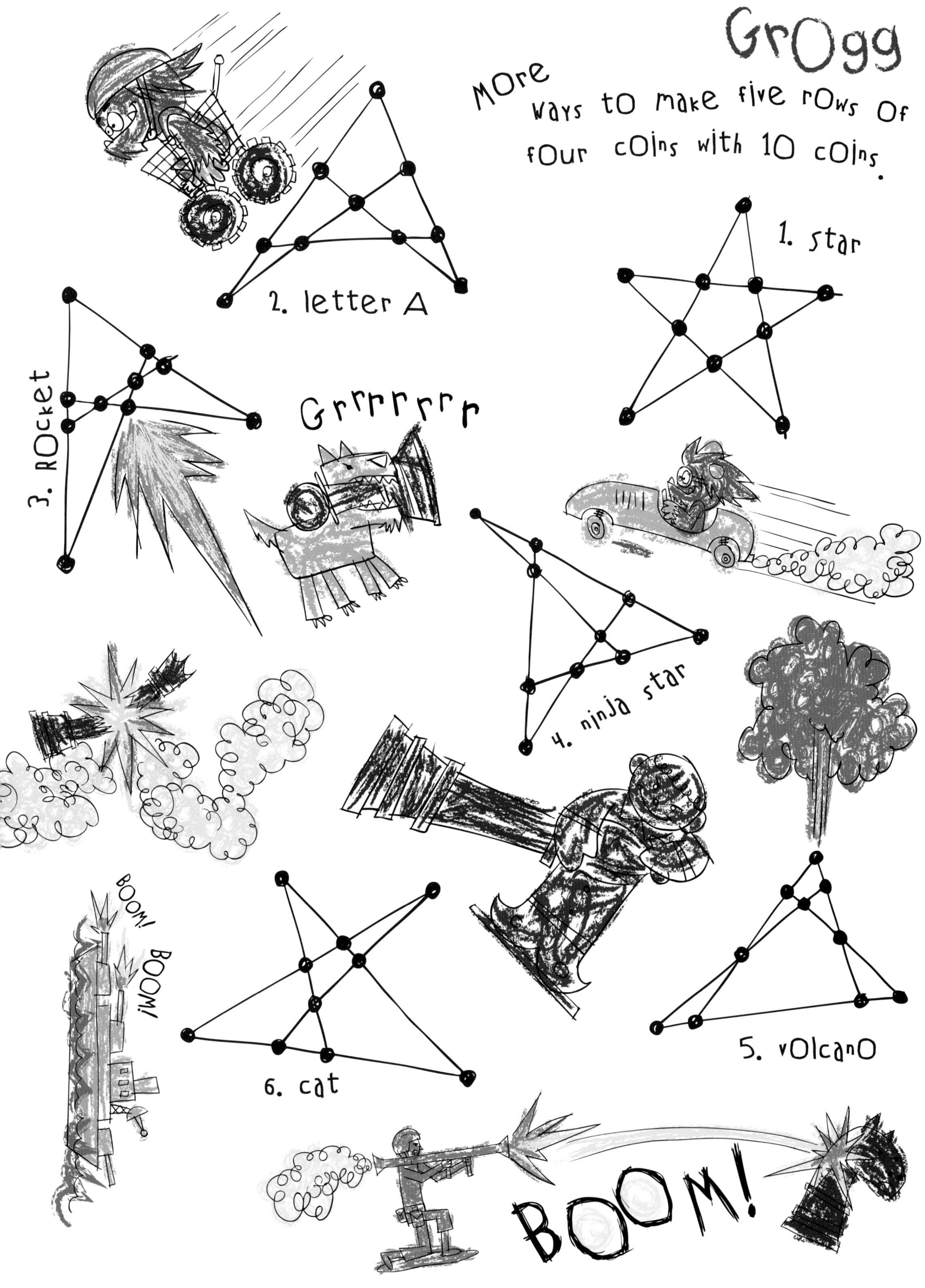
Grogg
MOre ways to make five rOws Of fOur cOins with 10 cOins.
1. star
2. letter A
3. ROcket
Grrrrrrr
4. ninja star
5. vOlcanO
6. cat
BOOM!
BOOM!
BOOM!

Contents: Chapter 5

See page 44 in the Practice book for a recommended reading/practice sequence for Chapter 5.

Chapter 5: Perfect Squares

Ms. Q.
Perfect Squares
Does everyone have enough graph paper?
Got it!
Yep.
I need another sheet, Ms. Q.
This little rectangle has a perimeter of 6.
Who can trace a shape that has a perimeter of *16*?
Made one!
Done.
Winnie
arf arf
Great! Now, find the ***area*** of your shape.
Whose shape has the largest area?
Find the areas of all four shapes.
Mine has fifteen squares.
Can anyone find a shape with a perimeter of 16 that has an area ***larger*** than 15?
Try it.

I can make my area bigger without changing its perimeter!
When I add another square to the bottom of my "W", my shape has one more square...
...but its perimeter is still 16!
Then you can add two ***more*** squares without changing the perimeter.
And six more here!
We filled in all the corners.
We turned your "W"...
...into a square!
Can you make it even ***bigger***?
There are no more corners to fill in.
Alex's ***rectangle*** doesn't have any corners to fill in either, but it's not as big as Winnie's square.
I know! If we cut off the top of Alex's rectangle...
...and put it here...
...the perimeter doesn't change!
But ***now*** we have a corner to fill in.
Is Winnie right? Check.

We get the same 4 by 4 square!
I think the square *is* the biggest shape you can trace that has a perimeter of 16!
I knew it!
It says here: "For a given perimeter, the largest rectilinear shape you can make is a square."*
*RECTILINEAR SHAPES ONLY HAVE RIGHT ANGLES.
That's right!
The square with perimeter **16** has area **16** squares.
What is the largest area we can trace with perimeter **20?**
20?
You can't just ***guess,*** Grogg!
All four sides of a square are the same length.
What number could we add four times to get 20?
5+5+5+5=20. If the side length of the big square is 5, the perimeter is 20...
...and the area is 5×5=**25** squares.
Good! Try one more. What is the largest area you can trace with perimeter 80?
Try it!

Groggasaurus!
RAWR!
We just make another square! All four sides are the same...
...and they have to add up to 80.
Four times what is 80?
Solve it.
4×2=8, so 4×20=80.
All four sides are 20, so the area is 20×20.
That's 2×2 with two extra zeros...
...400!
There is a special word for multiplying a number by itself...
...like 5×5, or 20×20. Can you guess what it is?
We're ***squaring*** the numbers!
That makes sense!
SQUARING A NUMBER MEANS MULTIPLYING IT BY ITSELF.
When you find the area of a square, you multiply a number by itself...
...and when you multiply a number by itself, you get a ***perfect square.***
That's why we call numbers like 16 and 25 perfect squares!
4×4=16, and 5×5=25.
A perfect square number of squares can make a square!

MATH TEAM
...with Fiona!

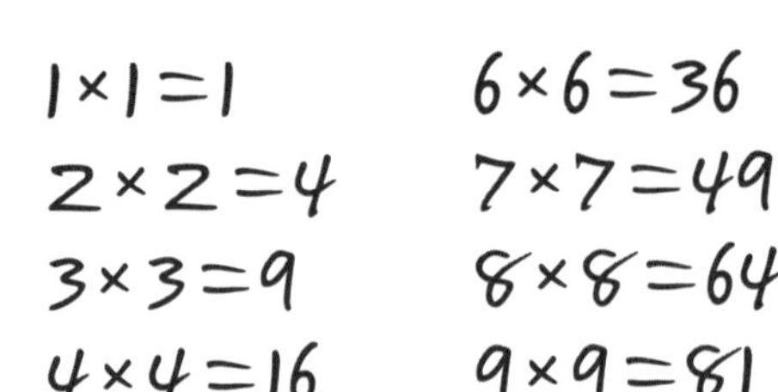
1×1=1
2×2=4
3×3=9
4×4=16
5×5=25
6×6=36
7×7=49
8×8=64
9×9=81
10×10=100
You already know your perfect squares up to 10×10. They make a diagonal on the times table.
Today, we'll learn to square some really big numbers!

Like 90!
90×90 is 9×9, but with two zeros at the end...
...8,100!

That's right. You all know how to square numbers that end in zero.
Try a few:
70×70 400×400 5,000×5,000 6,000,000×6,000,000

Try them.

70×70
400×400
5,000×5,000
6,000,000×6,000,000
=4,900
=160,000
=25,000,000
=36,000,000,000,000

Great. You can square big numbers that end in zero. Let's find a way to square numbers that end in 5.
Here are some numbers that end in 5. What do you notice about their squares?
15×15=225
25×25=625
35×35=1,225
45×45=2,025
55×55=3,025

What do you notice?

They all end in 25!

Right. If a number ends in 5, its square always ends in 25.

Great, but how do you get the part that comes *before* the 25?

Let's look.
Does anyone notice anything that will help us solve 65×65?
15×15=225
25×25=625
35×35=1,225
45×45=2,025
55×55=3,025
65×65=__25

I see a pattern.
If we erase all of the 5's and 25's, we get this...
A bunch of wrong answers?
Sure, but they're almost right.
1 ×1 =2 X
2 ×2 =6 X
3 ×3 =12 X
4 ×4 =20 X
5 ×5 =30 X
6 ×6 =__

See if you can find a pattern that will help you solve 65×65.

I see! If we add the number we are squaring, the *wrong* answers all become *right!*
1 ×1 +1 =2 ✓
2 ×2 +2 =6 ✓
3 ×3 +3 =12 ✓
4 ×4 +4 =20 ✓
5 ×5 +5 =30 ✓
6 ×6 =__

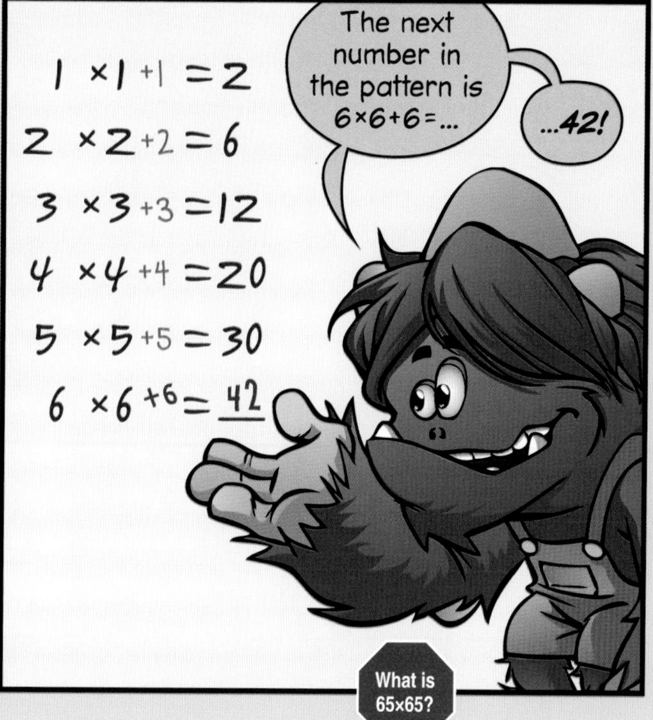
1 ×1 +1 =2
2 ×2 +2 =6
3 ×3 +3 =12
4 ×4 +4 =20
5 ×5 +5 =30
6 ×6 +6 = 42
The next number in the pattern is 6×6+6=...
...42!

What is 65×65?

Instead of 6×6+6, we can just multiply 6×7. They're the same.
Huh?
6×6 is six 6's. 6×6+6 is just one more 6, so that's seven 6's... 6×7.
Ahhh... So for 65×65, we multiply 6×7=42 and put a 25 on the end.
65×65 =4,225.
Why does *that* work?
Here's Professor Mumbles. He can explain.
Elttil ih sretsnom!
Evif-ytxis eht si derauqs 60+5 sa emas 60+5 semit...
...ew os eht tilps nac pu erauqs siht ekil...
...otni ruof seceip!
65
65
5
60
60
5
5
60
60
5
Elttil a tsuj htiw gnignarraer...
Aha! 65×65= 60×70+25.
Got it!
60×70=4,200, and we add 5×5=25 to get 4,225.
5
5
60
60
5
5
25
60
70

Practice: Pages 45-50

Ahoy, landlubbers!
By now, you've all finished buildin' your ships. 'Tis time to sew your sails.
Me first piratin' ship be havin' only one small sail...
Woodshop
SQUARING UP
...sixteen square patches sewn together to make one 4 by 4 square.
As me piratin' skills grew, so did me ship and her sails. I was always addin' more squares to embiggen me sail.
YEAH BUOY!
Each time I grew me sail, I added squares to the side and to the top.
To make me 4 by 4 sail into a 5 by 5 sail, I stitched a column of 4 squares on the side...
...and a row of 5 on top.
After addin' more squares, 'twas finally time to build a bigger ship and add a second sail.
Me new ship had one 10 by 10 sail and one 11 by 11 sail.
How many total squares be there in the bigger sail?
Try it!

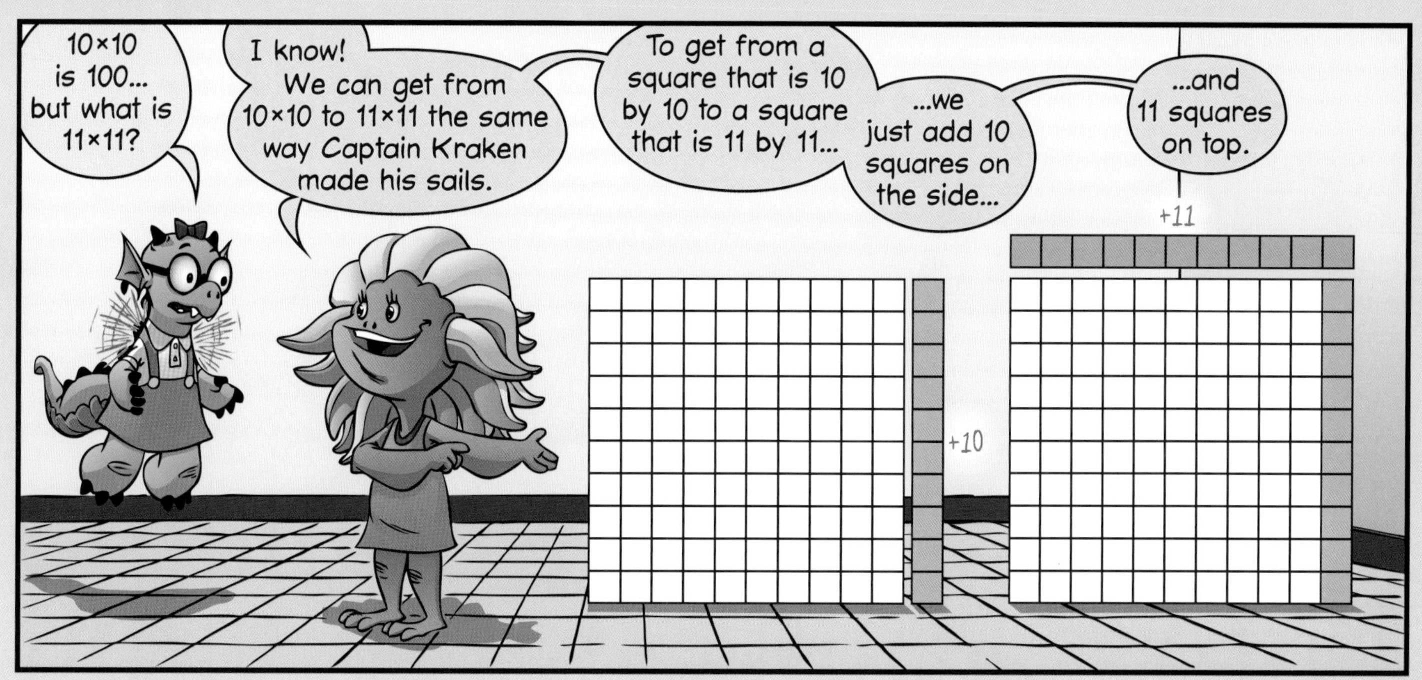
10×10 is 100... but what is 11×11?
I know! We can get from 10×10 to 11×11 the same way Captain Kraken made his sails.
To get from a square that is 10 by 10 to a square that is 11 by 11...
...we just add 10 squares on the side...
...and 11 squares on top.
+10
+11

So 11×11 is just 10×10+10+11.

That makes 100+10+11=121 squares in the larger sail!
Aye! 121 stitched squares.

Was it a fast ship?
She be a sleek 'n nimble ship, able to turn on a dime.
Fast? She made the Kessel Run in less than 12 parsecs!
Alas, she was a puny vessel compared to...

...the ***Angela Viathan***, the largest ship to ever sail the seven seas.
She had four masts, each holding six square sails. The smallest sail atop each mast was 40 squares wide and tall!
So the ***smallest*** sail was made from 40×40=***1,600*** fabric squares!
Each o' the two sails beneath it be one square wider 'n taller.
41 by 41?
Aye. What be the number o' fabric squares in a 41 by 41 sail?
Can you find the number of squares?
We already know 40 squared is 40×40=1,600.
To get from a 40×40 square to a 41×41 square, we just add 40 squares on the side and 41 on top...
...41 squared is 1,681!
40×40
= 1,600
+41
+40
41×41
= 1,600+40+41
= 1,600+81
= 1,681

So, if we know a perfect square, it's easy to find the ***next*** perfect square just by adding.
Aye. Try this. What be the square of 49?
Instead of adding, we can subtract!
We know that 50 squared is 2,500.
To get from 50 squared to 49 squared, we remove a row on top and a column on the side.
We just subtract 50 and 49 from 2,500!
-50
50×50 = 2,500
-49
49×49 = 2,500-50-49
Subtracting 50 and 49 is the same as subtracting 99...
...so 49 squared is 50×50 minus 99: 2,500-99 =2,401!
Very good!
Now, choose your fabric squares 'n' select a sew-bot.

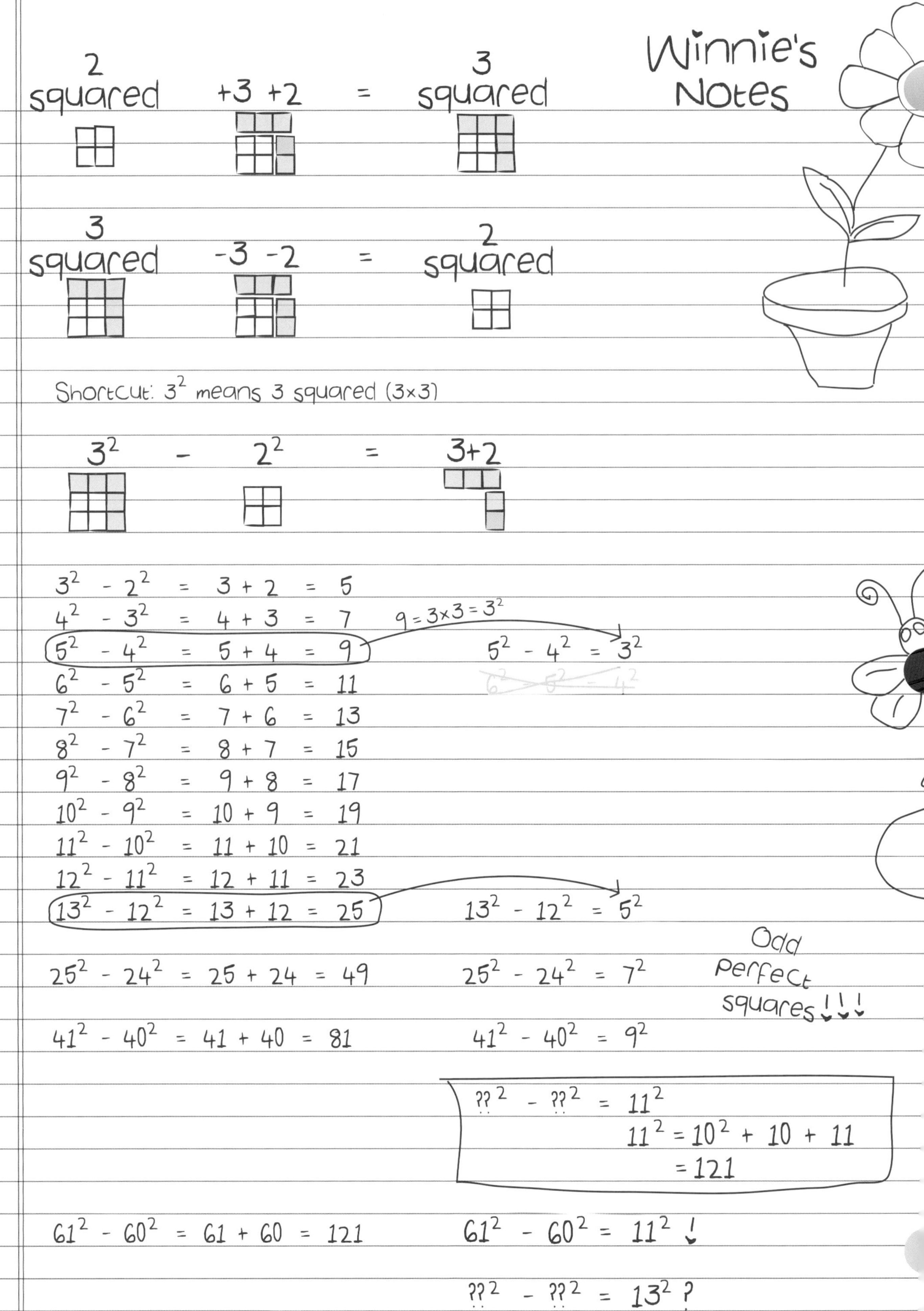

Winnie's Notes
2 squared +3 +2 = 3 squared
3 squared -3 -2 = 2 squared
Shortcut: 3^2 means 3 squared (3×3)
$3^2 - 2^2 = 3+2$
$3^2 - 2^2 = 3 + 2 = 5$
$4^2 - 3^2 = 4 + 3 = 7$
$9 = 3 \times 3 = 3^2$
$5^2 - 4^2 = 5 + 4 = 9$
$5^2 - 4^2 = 3^2$
$6^2 - 5^2 = 6 + 5 = 11$
$7^2 - 6^2 = 7 + 6 = 13$
$8^2 - 7^2 = 8 + 7 = 15$
$9^2 - 8^2 = 9 + 8 = 17$
$10^2 - 9^2 = 10 + 9 = 19$
$11^2 - 10^2 = 11 + 10 = 21$
$12^2 - 11^2 = 12 + 11 = 23$
$13^2 - 12^2 = 13 + 12 = 25$
$13^2 - 12^2 = 5^2$
$25^2 - 24^2 = 25 + 24 = 49$
$25^2 - 24^2 = 7^2$
Odd perfect squares!!!
$41^2 - 40^2 = 41 + 40 = 81$
$41^2 - 40^2 = 9^2$
$??^2 - ??^2 = 11^2$
$11^2 = 10^2 + 10 + 11$
$= 121$
$61^2 - 60^2 = 61 + 60 = 121$
$61^2 - 60^2 = 11^2$!
$??^2 - ??^2 = 13^2$?

Dots and Boxes

Instructions:

Start with a grid of dots like the one below. The grid may be any size.

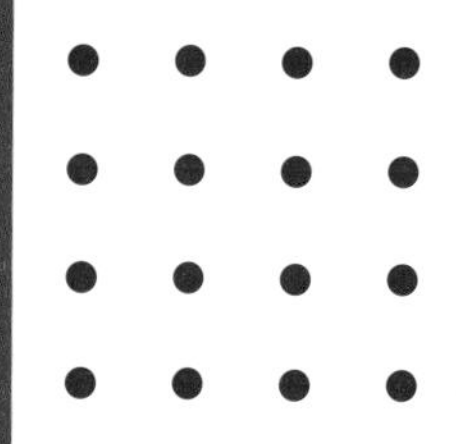

The Beginning: Players take turns connecting a neighboring pair of dots with a horizontal or vertical line. Below are the first three moves in a sample game between Alex and Winnie.

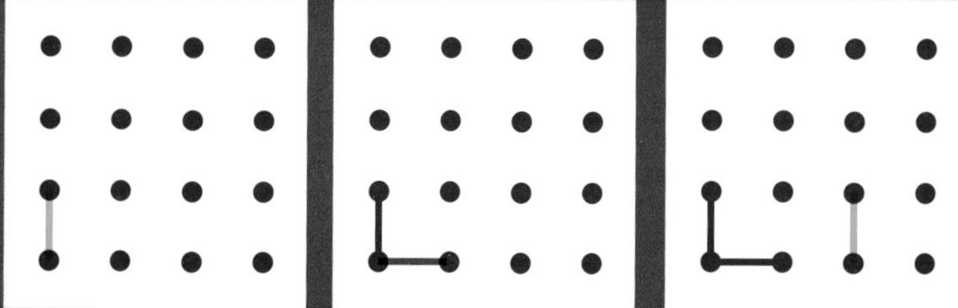

The Middle: When a player completes the fourth side of a small square, he or she "wins" the square and places his or her initial inside it, then takes another turn as shown below.

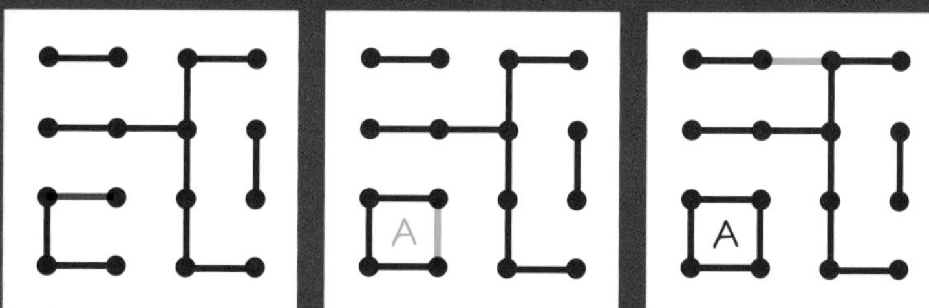

The End: The game ends when all the squares have been completed. The player with the most squares wins.

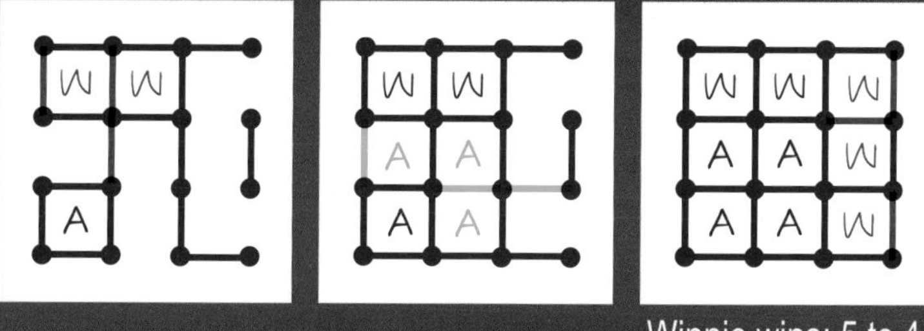

Winnie wins: 5 to 4.

R & G
In the Garden
What are we planting today?
Snapdragons!
SNAP!
SNAP!
SNAP!
Yow!
SNAP!

They come in 9 colors!
1 Black snapdragon
3 Pink snapdragons
5 periwinkle snapdragons
7 Orange snapdragons
9 Blue snapdragons
11 Green snapdragons
13 purple snapdragons
15 Yellow snapdragons
17 Red snapdragons
Those are odd.

That's what makes them so cute!
I suppose, but what I meant was that you bought an ***odd*** number of each color. How come?
SNAP!

I'm planting them in that corner back there.
I made a planting chart to see how many of each color I should buy.
17 red
15 yellow
13 purple
11 green
9 blue
7 orange
5 periwinkle
3 pink
1 black

So there are 81 flowers all together.
Hmmm...
1 plus 3 is 4,
plus 5 is 9,
plus 7 is 16,
plus 9 is 25...
...wait,
how did you add all of these numbers so fast?!
SNAP! SNAP!
Do you know how he counted so fast?

I didn't!
I **squared** 9.
!?!
Look at your chart again.

I see, it's a **square!** Nine rows of nine makes 9×9=81 snapdragons.

So, to add the first 9 **odd** numbers, you can just square 9.
To add the first 10 odd numbers, can you just square 10?

To make a 10 by 10 square, you would need to buy 19 more flowers.
That would make a total of 100 snapdragons!
19
17
15
13
11
9
7
5
3
1

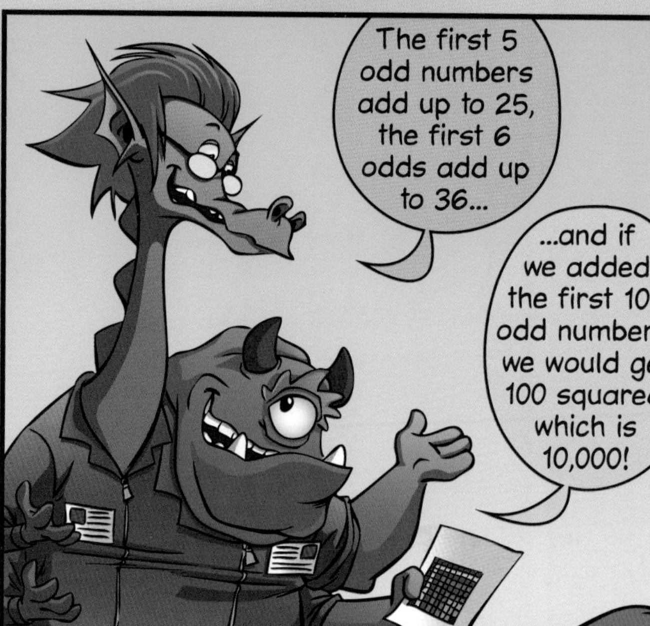
The first 5 odd numbers add up to 25, the first 6 odds add up to 36...
...and if we added the first 100 odd numbers, we would get 100 squared, which is 10,000!

Uh oh.
What's wrong?
Maybe we shouldn't have planted the snapdragons so close to the tiger lilies.
SNAP!

Practice: Pages 51-58

THE LAB
DISSECTIONS
Today, we'll be dissecting...

...squares!
sigh

DISSECT MEANS TO SEPARATE INTO SMALLER PIECES. IN THIS LESSON WE DISSECT SQUARES INTO SMALLER SQUARES.

You've all been learning about perfect squares.

Any square can be dissected into a perfect square number of smaller squares that are all the same size.

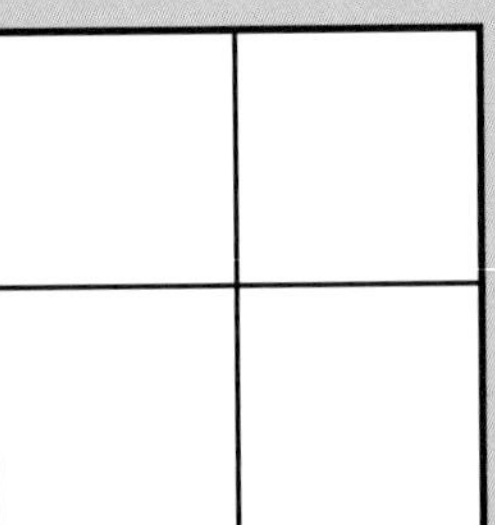
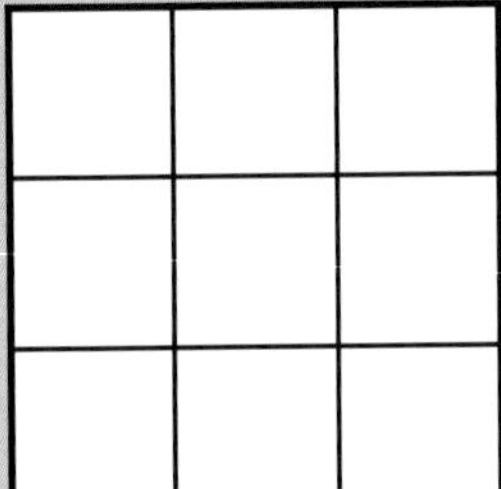
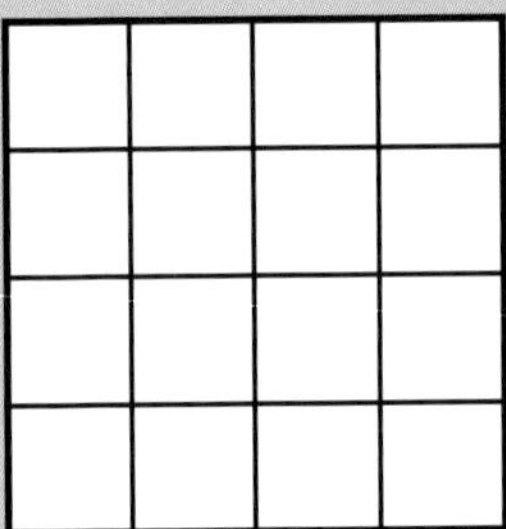
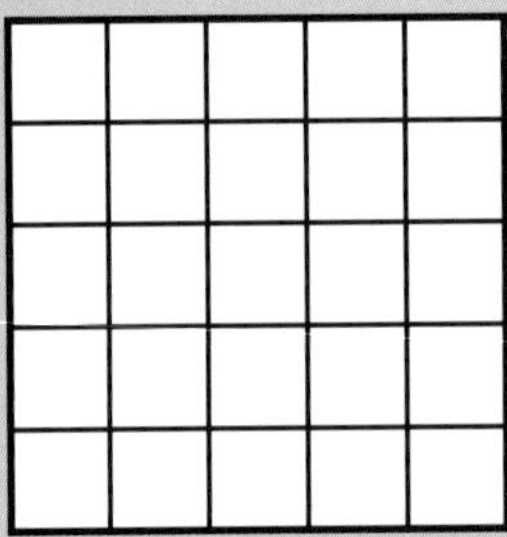

Today we will try to divide a square into smaller squares that are ***not*** all the same size. Let's start with a small one.

Tracing the lines of the grid, how could we divide a 3 by 3 perfect square into ***six*** smaller squares instead of nine?

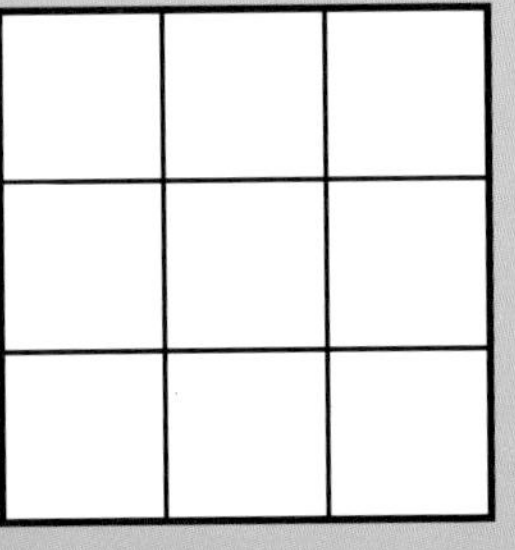

You can take four of the little squares and make a big one.

THESE SQUARE DISSECTIONS ARE CALLED "MRS. PERKINS'S QUILTS."

That's right!
Next, try dissecting a 5 by 5 square into smaller squares. What is the smallest number of squares you can make?
I got 8 squares.
I got 8.
Me too.
Your answers all look different!
You're all right! One 3×3 square, three 2×2 squares, and four 1×1 squares makes 8 squares all together, and there are lots of ways to rearrange them...
...but you cannot dissect the 5 by 5 square into fewer than 8 smaller squares.
Next, try dissecting the 7 by 7 square into as few squares as possible.
Print more blank squares at BeastAcademy.com
What is the smallest number of squares you can use for the 7 by 7 square?

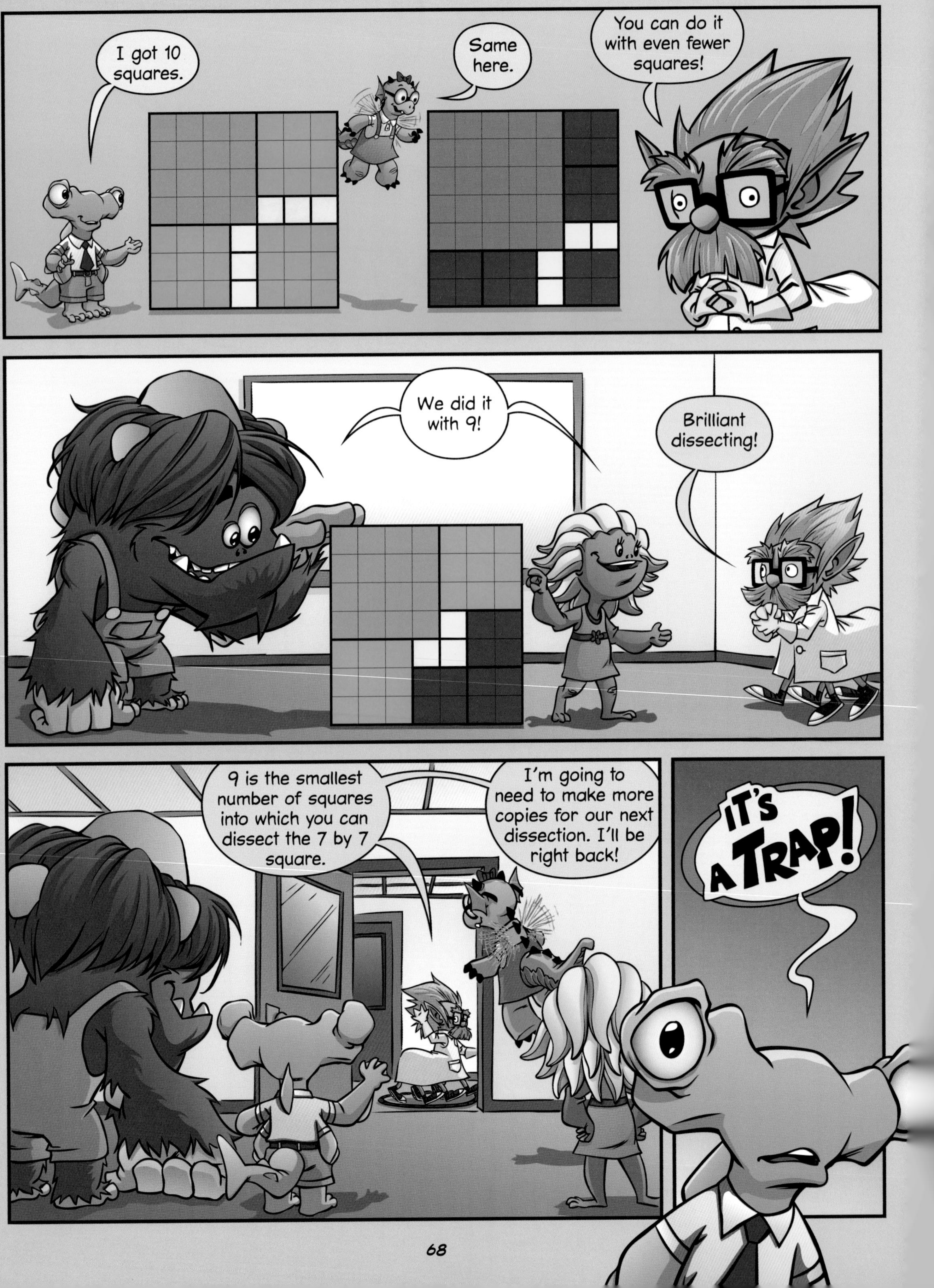

9 is the smallest number of squares into which you can dissect the 7 by 7 square.

I'm going to need to make more copies for our next dissection. I'll be right back!

IT'S A TRAP!

Bwah Ha Ha! Professor Grok is gone. I've abducted your educator. It's time for some...
...Diabolical Dissections!
Dissecting a five by five square is perfectly pedestrian. Slicing the seven by seven square is certainly simple. But the devious dissection I demand is...
...Devastatingly Difficult!!!
A tricky tracing of this thirteen by thirteen square separates it into eleven squares.
Slip a sheet with the solution into the reading room and I will release your renowned rhetorician. Fail to do so, and I will...
...Demand His Dissection!!!
We need to dissect a 13×13 square into only ***eleven*** smaller squares?!
Is that even possible?
On the easier problems, we always had a big square in the top left corner.
We should try that.
Lizzie and I will start with a 7 by 7 square in the top left corner. Winnie and Grogg, you start with an 8 by 8 square.
Try to find a way to dissect the 13 by 13 square into 11 smaller squares.
Print more blank squares at BeastAcademy.com

I found a way to get 11!

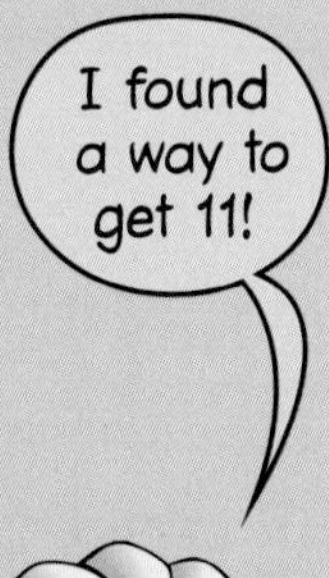

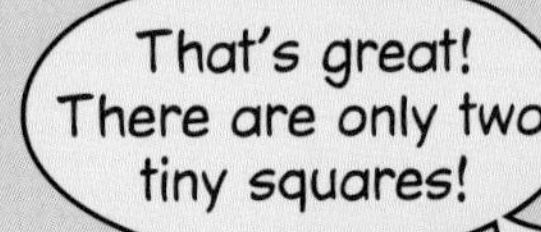

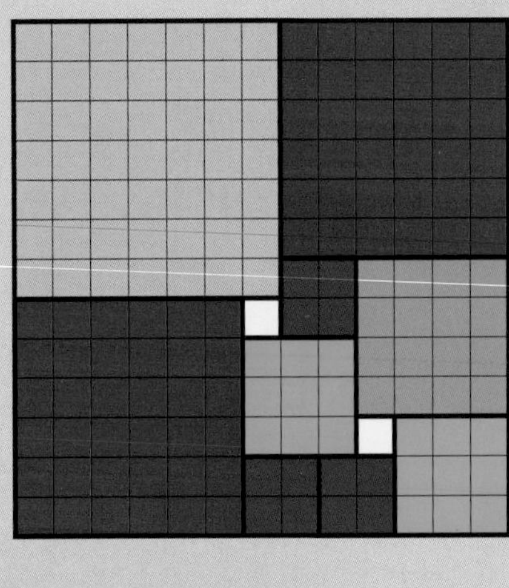

To the reading room!

TITLE 89×89 Square Dissection	
NAME Alex	DATE 12/5

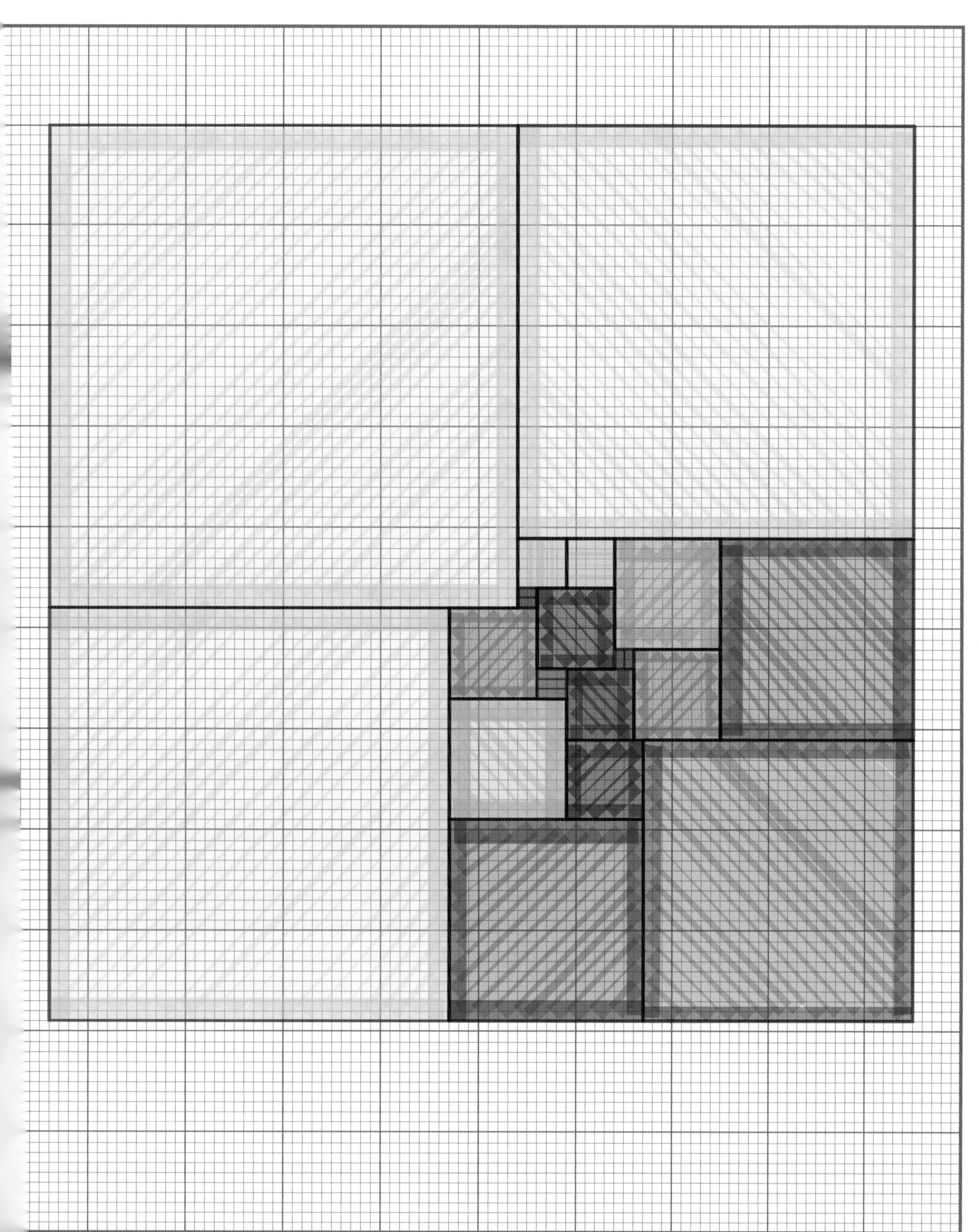

Contents: Chapter 6

See page 74 in the Practice book for a recommended reading/practice sequence for Chapter 6.

Chapter 6:
The Distributive Property

R & G
Order of Operations

Hey!
Huh?

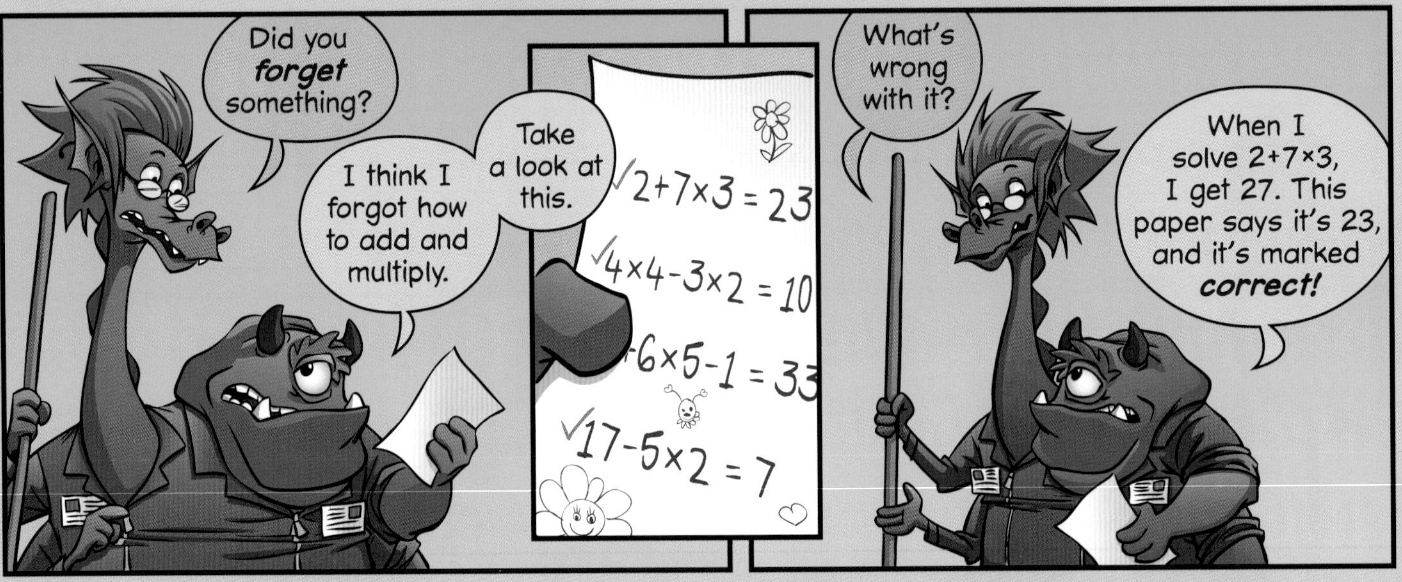
Did you *forget* something?
I think I forgot how to add and multiply.
Take a look at this.
2+7×3 = 23
4×4-3×2 = 10
6×5-1 = 33
17-5×2 = 7
What's wrong with it?
When I solve 2+7×3, I get 27. This paper says it's 23, and it's marked *correct!*

Let me try again.
I add 2+7 to get 9, then multiply by 3 to get 27.
I see your problem. You *added* before you *multiplied.*
Of course I added before I multiplied. The addition was *first!*
2+7×3
= 9×3
= 27

Yes, but there are rules for solving math problems.* You don't *always* go from left to right.
In problems without parentheses, we multiply before we add or subtract.
2+7×3
= 9×3
= 27
2+7×3
= 2+21
= 23

*THESE RULES ARE CALLED THE *ORDER OF OPERATIONS.*

Why can't we just work from left to right?
Try this... Remember our cousin Horatio?
We call him "Spike."
Right. He's covered with them.
He **scares** me.
Horatio has three tails, each with 7 spikes.
He also has four shoulder plates, each with 2 spikes.
How many spikes does Horatio have all together?
Let's see. He has three tails, each with 7 spikes...
...plus four shoulder plates, each with 2 spikes.
3×7 + 4×2
= 21 + 8
= 29
That's 29 spikes!
That's right, but look what you did. You didn't work from left to right, you multiplied first!
You're right! I found the number of tail spikes, then I found the number of shoulder spikes, and I added those two numbers together.
That makes sense. If you just work from left to right, you get the **wrong** answer.
3×7 + 4×2
= 21 + 8
= 29
3×7+4×2

You get two different answers. They can't **both** be correct.
That's why we need a rule!

Right! In ancient times, math beasts decided that we multiply before we add or subtract.

Does addition come before subtraction?
Nope.
After multiplying, you add and subtract from left to right.

Ahhh! Let me try these problems again.

2+7×3
= 2+21
= 23

4×4−3×2
= 16 − 6
= 10

4+6×5−1
= 4+30−1
= 34−1
= 33

17−5×2
= 17−10
= 7

Nice work! How about this one...
...remember the tiger lilies we planted last month?
They started a turf war with the snapdragons!

We planted ten lilies, and each one had four petals.
Sure. Each lily grew three more petals...
...but two lilies uprooted and moved to the park.

How many total petals are on the tiger lilies we have left?
We multiply the number of lilies we have left: 10-2...
...times the number of petals on each lily: 4+3.

Practice: Pages 75-77

Ms. Q.

Big Rectangles

Have you all finished drawing your rectangles?

Here's mine.

Almost done... ...I want to make sure my lines are straight.

Rectangle?

I drew a tangled wreck.

Can you find the area of your rectangles?

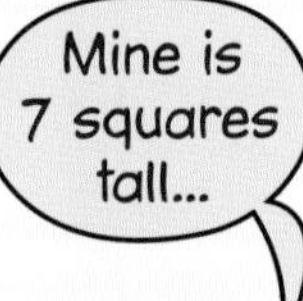
Mine is 7 squares tall...

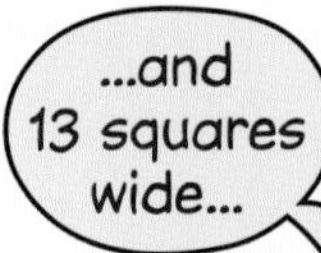
...and 13 squares wide...

. . .

...so I need to multiply 7 times 13.

What could we do to make finding the area of Lizzie's rectangle easier?

Can you think of a way to make finding the area easier?

What if we split Lizzie's rectangle into two smaller rectangles?
We can find the areas of both small rectangles.
Then, we can just add those areas together!
Great idea!
What is the best way to split Lizzie's rectangle in two?
How would you split it?
This line separates her 7 by 13 rectangle into two rectangles.
One is 7 by 10, and the other is 7 by 3.
Both of *those* areas are easy to figure out!
7
10
3
7×10 is 70.
7×3 is 21.
So 7×13 is 70+21=91!
Do mine! Do mine!
My rectangle is 3 by ummm...
...52!
Can you find the area of Grogg's rectangle?

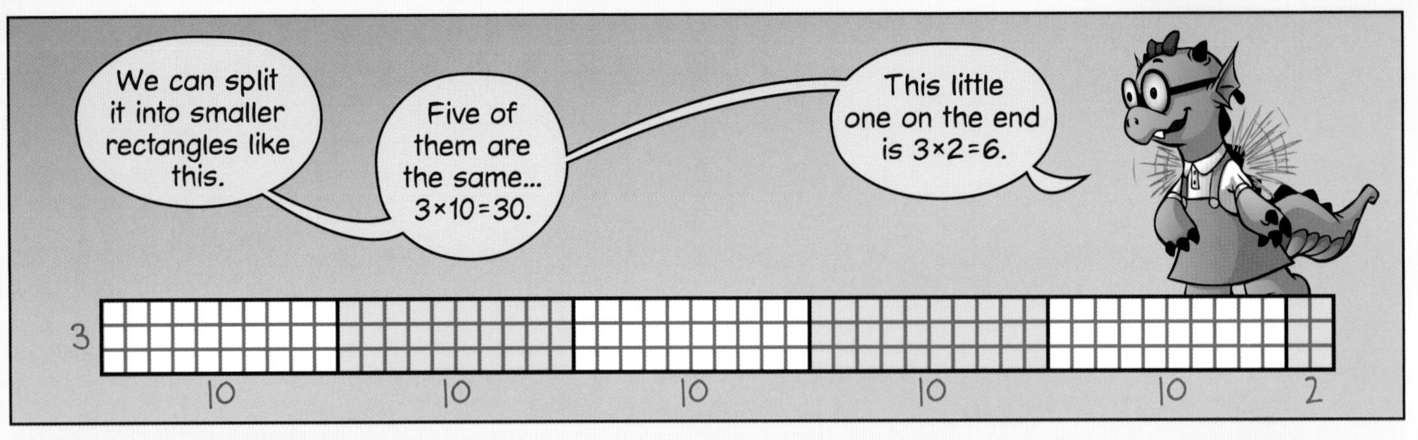
We can split it into smaller rectangles like this.
Five of them are the same... 3×10=30.
This little one on the end is 3×2=6.
3
10
10
10
10
10
2

So the five big rectangles have a total of 5×30=150 squares...
...plus these six on the end makes 156 total!
5×30=150
3×2=6

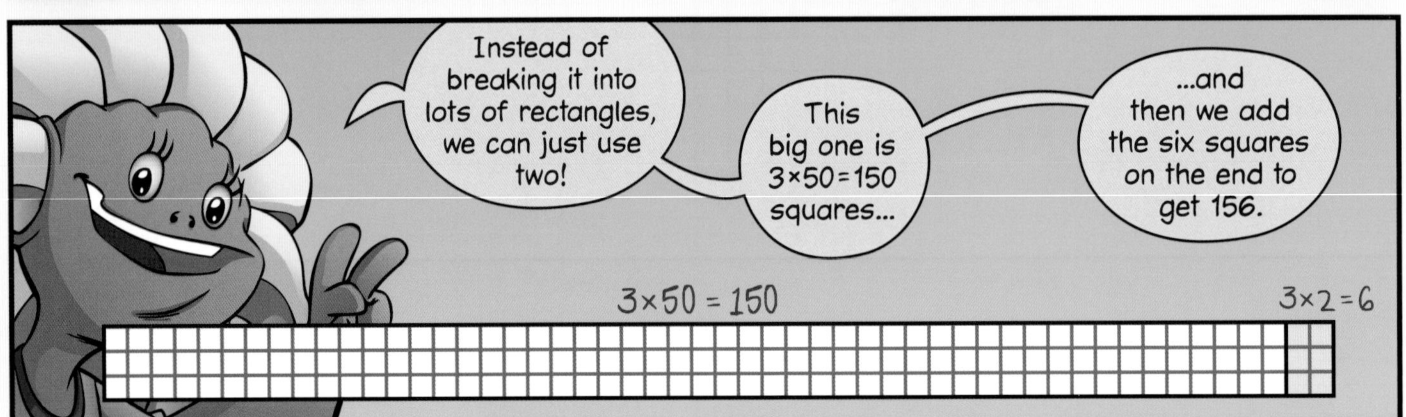
Instead of breaking it into lots of rectangles, we can just use two!
This big one is 3×50=150 squares...
...and then we add the six squares on the end to get 156.
3×50 = 150
3×2=6

It doesn't matter how you split up the rectangle, as long as you remember to add all the pieces to get the total area.

And when you split it into pieces, it is usually best to use ***multiples*** of 10.
Very good! Who's next?
Me! My rectangle is 9 by 18.

WHEN YOU MULTIPLY A NUMBER BY 10, THE NUMBER YOU GET IS CALLED A ***MULTIPLE*** OF 10. FOR EXAMPLE, THE NUMBERS 10, 60, AND 140 ARE ALL ***MULTIPLES*** OF 10.

How would you split Winnie's rectangle to find its area?

You can split it into one rectangle that is 9 by 10, and one that is 9 by 8.
9×10=90
9×8=72
If we add these two areas together, we get 90+72=162!
90+72=162
I did it differently. You can split the rectangle in half.
That makes two 9 by 9 squares...
9×9=81
9×9=81
...and doubling 81 gives us 162.
81×2 = 162
I guess you don't *always* need to use multiples of ten.
Not always, but it's *usually* a good idea. Can we find the area of yours next, Alex?
Sure. Mine is really easy!
Why is that?
It's a perfect 10 by 10 square.

Workshop
PIRATE BOOTY
Shiver me timbers! You little monsters have all finished your sailin' ships!

'Tis time to christen your ships 'n set sail for a maiden voyage!
Squawk. Bon voyage!

Each of your ships will be loaded with treasure. If there be one thing every pirate ship needs, 'tis a hull full o' pirate booty!
Snicker Snicker

In this chest be gold doubloons of varyin' worth. Your goal be to transport coins 'cross the school fountain.
I don't think these are real gold.
Arrrr! They taste like chocolate!
Real gold doubloons don't have big numbers and smiley faces on them.
Each coin be stamped with a number tellin' you its worth. The bigger coins be worth more than the smaller ones. Choose a coin 'n start loadin' your ships.

I'll use these little 3's.

I'll use 7's.

I'll take the 9's!

Arrrrr! I'll load these 18's onto the SS Denominator.

Set sail, little buccaneers!
Grogg! Is your ship ***biting*** mine?!
Aye, you lily-livered landlubber! Prepare to be plundered!
Quit it! Give me that!

Time to tally your treasure 'n figure whose haul be worth the most.

My ship carried fifty-one of these 3's.

I have twenty-three 7's...

...I'm sure I loaded 25.

My ship carried nineteen 9's!

Arrrr! The SS Denominator hauled seven 18's...

...and plundered two 7's from the Coral Princess.

Can you figure out whose treasure is worth the most?

I'm not used to multiplying such big numbers.
Let's see, what is 3×51?

Arrrr! I'll make it easy! Hand over a coin, scurvy reptile!
Why?
Then, you'll have only 50 coins... and 3×50 is easy!

That's right! If I take one coin away, it's easy to multiply 3×50=150. Then, I can add the coin back to get 150+3=153!
My coins are worth 153!

Aye. Multiplyin' 3×51 be the same as multiplyin' 3×50 and addin' one more 3.
Now, what be the value of your twenty-three 7's, Winnie?

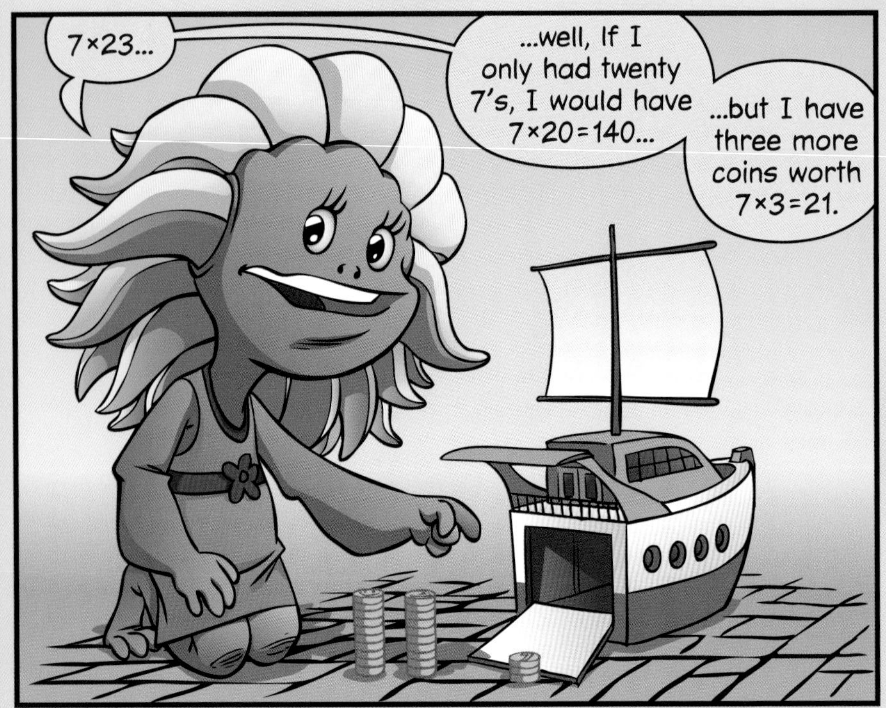
7×23...
...well, If I only had twenty 7's, I would have 7×20=140...
...but I have three more coins worth 7×3=21.

That makes the total value of all 23 coins 140+21=161!

'Tis the ***distributive property!***
7×23 be equal to 7×20 plus 7×3.
Twenty-three 7's is the same as twenty 7's plus three 7's.

Aye. What be the value of your treasure, Alex?
My ship carried nineteen 9's.

If I had ten 9's, that would make 90. Nine more 9's is 81. Added together, I get...
...90+81 =171.
Arrrr! There be an easier way!

What if you had twenty 9's and I plundered one?
I get it! 9×20=180, so to solve 9×19, I can just take away a 9... 180-9=171!
That ***is*** easier!
9

Aye. Excellent figurin'! Now, we'll examine Grogg's booty.

Oh, my ***treasure!***
'Tis a mighty haul! Seven 18's and two 7's.
How much is Grogg's treasure worth?

'Tis a troublesome task. 7×18 is 7×10 plus 7×8, then we add these two 7's...
Arrrr! I've lost track. Be there an easier way?
I know. We can trade Grogg's seven 18's for eighteen of my 7's.

Hands off, ***scallywag!***
They're worth the same, because 18×7=7×18!

All right, but I'll be keepin' me good eye on you.

If we add the two 7's he stole from ***my*** ship to the eighteen 7's here, that makes twenty 7's, or 20×7=140!

Arrrr! 'Tis the smallest haul of them all...

...I've failed as a pirate.

Don't beat yourself up about it, lad. Proper plunderin' takes plenty o' practice.

Practice: Pages 78-80

MATH TEAM
...with Fiona!

The semester's final math meet is this afternoon. We need to cover one important thing...
...the **distributive property.**
It's good for multiplying big numbers.

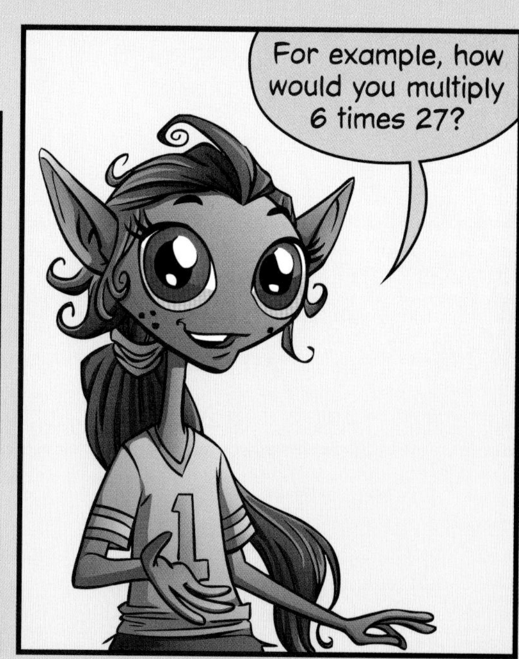

For example, how would you multiply 6 times 27?

You could start with 6 times 20, then add 6 times 7.
6×27
6×20
6×7
120
42
162
6×20 is 120, and 6×7 is 42...
...so 6 times 27 is 120+42=162!

Great! You just used the distributive property!

Since 27 is the same as 20+7...
...6×27 equals 6×(20+7).
6×27
= 6×(20+7)

*REMEMBER TO USE PARENTHESES! 6×20+7 IS NOT THE SAME AS 6×27.

We can rewrite 6×(20+7) as 6×20+6×7.
This is called **distributing** the 6.
We multiply the 6 by the numbers we are adding inside the parentheses.
6×27
= 6×(20+7)
= 6×20+6×7

THE DISTRIBUTIVE PROPERTY TELLS US THAT 6×(20+7) IS EQUAL TO 6×20+6×7, SO WE CAN REWRITE 6×(20+7) AS 6×20+6×7.

Then, we add.
6×27
= 6×(20+7)
= 6×20+6×7
= 120+42
= 162

It's just like when we found the areas of big rectangles!
And when we counted our pirate treasure!
How would you solve this one?
41×8
Try it!

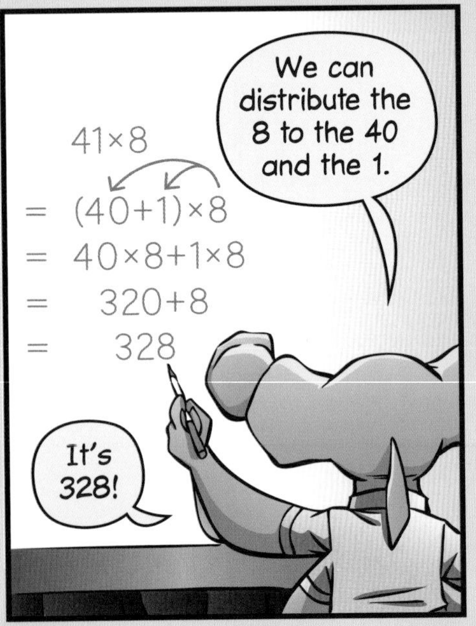
We can distribute the 8 to the 40 and the 1.
41×8
= (40+1)×8
= 40×8+1×8
= 320+8
= 328
It's 328!

Good! Try this one.
7×29

7×29
= 7×(20+9)
= 7×20+7×9
= 140+63
= 203
203!

How did you know 140+63 so fast?
Because 140+63 is the same as 140+60+3.
140+63
= 140+60+3
= 200+3
= 203

What about solving 7×29 this way?
7×29
= 7×(30-1)
= 7×30-7×1
= 210-7
= 203

Both ways work. You can replace the 29 with (20+9), or with (30-1), because they both equal 29.

Let's try something different.
How would you solve 17×5+3×5?

17×5 is the same as seventeen 5's...
...and 3×5 is three 5's.
We can add seventeen 5's plus three 5's to get twenty 5's!
20×5 is 100!
What does this have to do with the distributive property?

It *is* the distributive property!
Since we can rewrite (17+3)×5 as 17×5+3×5...

WHEN YOU USE THE DISTRIBUTIVE PROPERTY TO WRITE 17×5+3×5 AS (17+3)×5, IT IS CALLED ***FACTORING.***

...we can also change 17×5+3×5 to (17+3)×5...
...which is just 20×5=100!
= 17×5+3×5
= (17+3)×5
= 20×5
= 100

Try this one...
...what do you get when you add nine 1's plus nine 2's plus nine 3's plus nine 4's?

9×1 + 9×2 + 9×3 + 9×4

90!
9×1 + 9×2 + 9×3 + 9×4
= 9 + 18 + 27 + 36
Can you find the shortcut that Winnie used?

9×1 + 9×2 + 9×3 + 9×4
= 9 + 18 + 27 + 36
3
9
18
27
+36
90
She's right! How did you get that so fast, Winnie?

9×1 + 9×2 + 9×3 + 9×4
= 9×(1+2+3+4)
= 9×10
= 90
Instead of multiplying first and then adding, I rewrote the problem using the distributive property.

So, for this problem...
8×9+8×10+8×11

...instead of solving it this way...
8×9+8×10+8×11
= 72 + 80 + 88
= 152 + 88
= 240
11
152
+88
240

...I can rewrite it like this!
8×9+8×10+8×11
= 8×(9+10+11)
= 8×(30)
= 240

And now...
Time for the math meet.
Good luck!
...please welcome the Little Monsters of Beast Academy and their opponents, the Bots!

Practice: Pages 81-88

Today's math meet will consist of 6 questions...
...covering all the topics you have learned so far this year.*
The first five questions are each worth one point. The final question is worth two. The team with the most points wins the meet. Is everyone ready?
Question 1: A scalene triangle has whole number side lengths. One side has length 2, and another has length 3. What is the perimeter of the triangle?
Try it!
*THIS INCLUDES TOPICS COVERED IN GUIDE AND PRACTICE 3A.
We need to know the third side of the triangle.
The triangle is scalene, so all three sides have to be different lengths.
So the third side can't be 2 or 3...
...can it be 1?
1 is too short... 1+2=3.
See page 83 of Guide 3A to review the Triangle Inequality.
That means the third side has to be more than 3. The unknown side is the longest side of the triangle.
The short sides are 2 and 3...
...so the long side has to be less than 2+3=5.
It has to be 4!
Is 4 the correct answer to question 1?

The perimeter is 2+3+4=9.
DING!

Nine is correct! The Monsters take the early lead: one to zero.
Question 2: Compute 6×5×4×3×2×1.

We can ignore the 1. Multiplying a number by 1 gives us the number.
6×5×4×3×2

We can pair the 2 and the 5 to make 10, since multiplying by 10 is easy.
6×4×3×(2×5)
= 6×4×3 × 10

We should start with 6×3 to get 18.
(6×3)×4×10
= 18 ×4×10

Then, we can double twice to multiply by 4!
18×4×10
= 18×2×2×10

18×2 is 36, 36×2 is 72, and--
BZZZZZT!
720.
Correct! Bots tie the score at 1.

4
7
8
2
3
10
Question 3: Each team has been given a rectilinear shape with the dimensions shown. The shape can be cut into two pieces that can then be rearranged to form a square. What is the side length of the square?
Try it!
The bots are already cutting their shape!
I don't think we actually need to know how to cut it into two pieces that make a square.
Maybe there is an easier way to solve the problem.
SKRATCH SKRATCH
Do you see an easier way?

If we find the area of the original shape...
It's the same as the area of the square!
Because rearranging the pieces doesn't change the area of a shape!

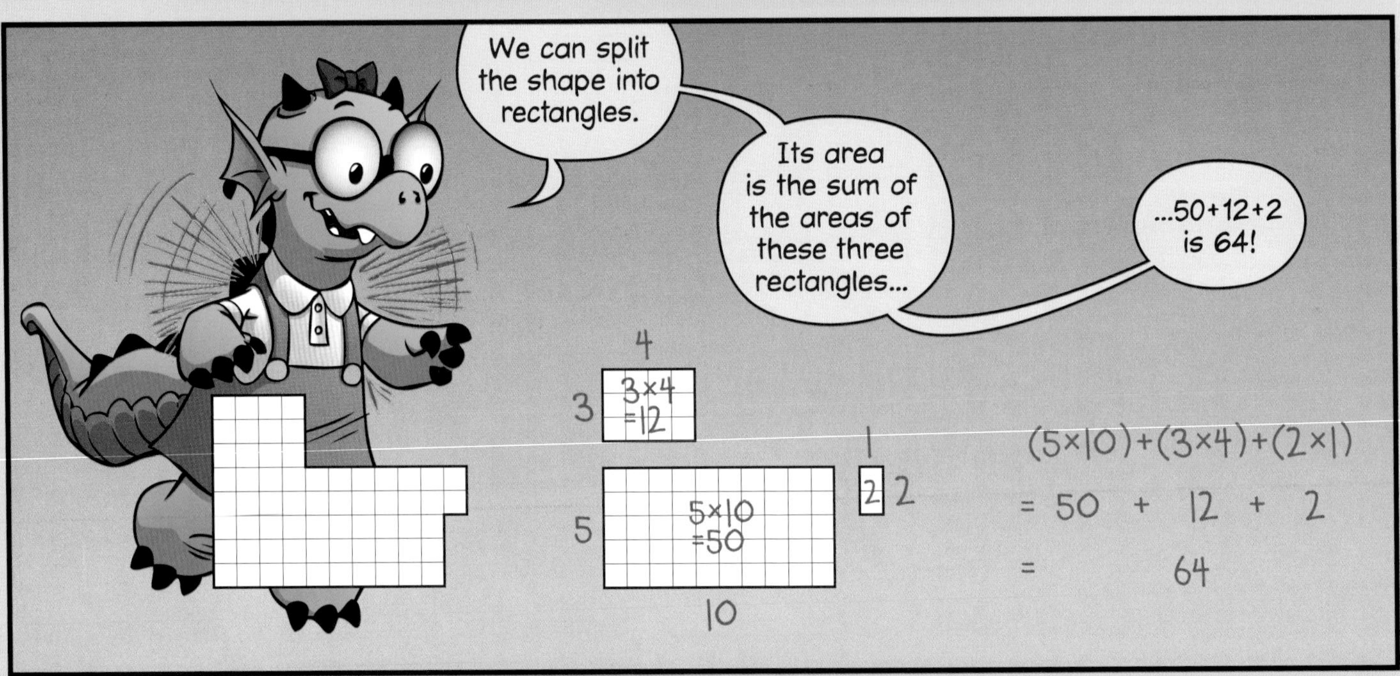
We can split the shape into rectangles.
Its area is the sum of the areas of these three rectangles...
...50+12+2 is 64!
4
3
3×4 =12
5
5×10 =50
10
1
2
2
(5×10)+(3×4)+(2×1)
= 50 + 12 + 2
= 64

The area of the square is 64!
Since 8×8=64, the side length of the square is...
...8!
DING!
Correct! The Little Monsters retake the lead, 2 to 1!
Can you find the two pieces that can be rearranged to make an 8×8 square?

Question 4:
Rick skip-counts by 7's, starting at 7. Nick skip-counts by 9's, starting at 9. What is the only 2-digit number that Rick and Nick will both say?
BZZZZZZT!
Huh!?
Try it!

63.
Correct!

Of course! 63 is 7×9...
...or 9×7.
It's seven 9's...
...or nine 7's.

The score is tied again, with just two questions left.

Question 5:
Compute (1×44)+(3×44)+(5×44)+(7×44)+(9×44).

Try it!

We can use the distributive property!

One 44 plus three 44's plus five 44's plus seven 44's plus nine 44's...
...is the same as (1+3+5+7+9)×44!

$$1\times44 + 3\times44 + 5\times44 + 7\times44 + 9\times44 = (1+3+5+7+9)\times44$$

1+3+5+7+9! That's the sum of the first five odd numbers!
The sum of the first five odd numbers is 5 squared... 25!
(1+3+5+7+9)×44
=25×44

SEE PAGES 64–65 FOR REVIEW.

Now we just need to multiply 25×44.
I got it!

What is it!?!
I cut two pieces that can be rearranged to make a square!
Grogg! That was ten minutes ago! We need to multiply 25×44!

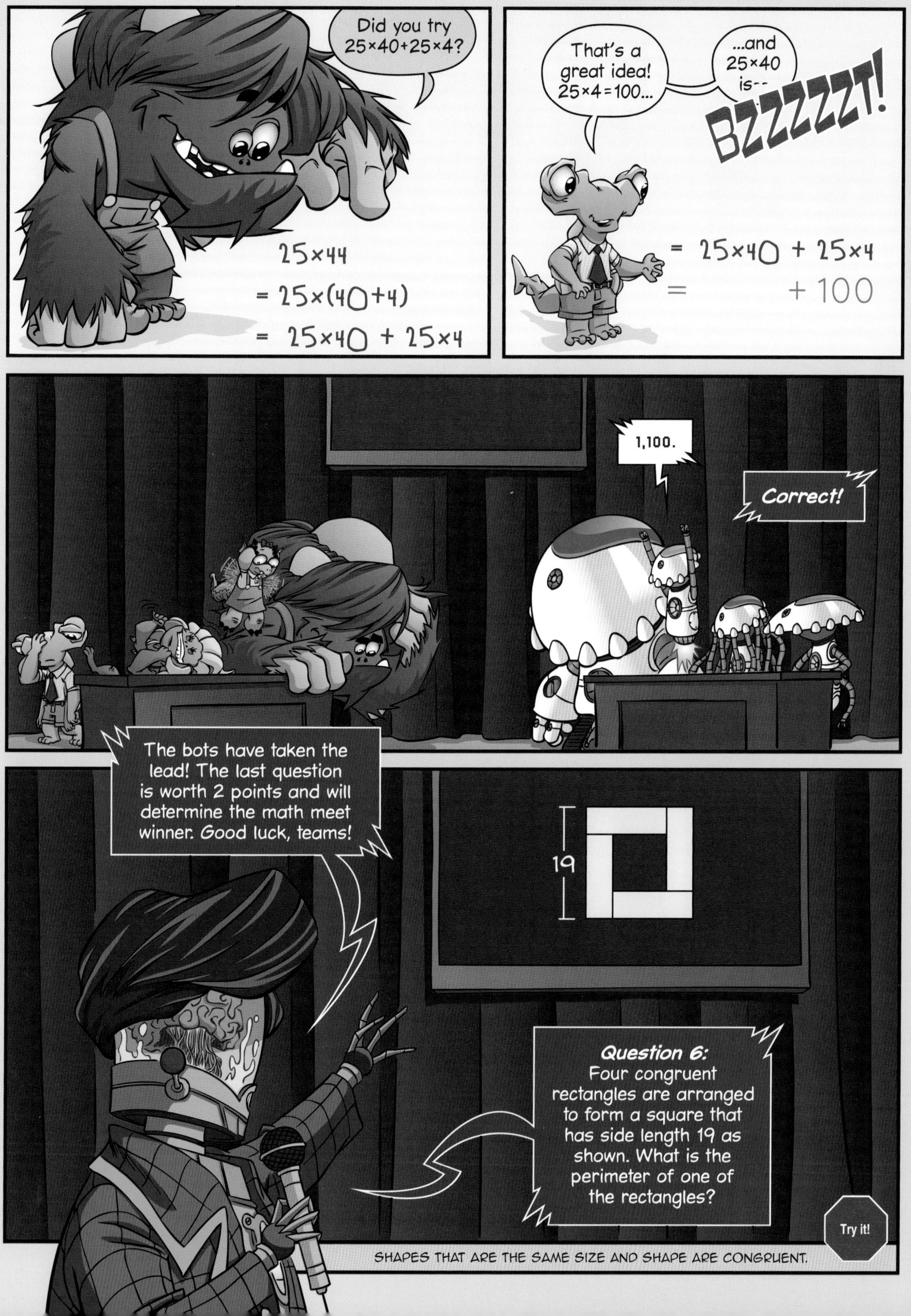

1,100.

Correct!

The bots have taken the lead! The last question is worth 2 points and will determine the math meet winner. *Good luck, teams!*

19

Question 6:
Four congruent rectangles are arranged to form a square that has side length 19 as shown. What is the perimeter of one of the rectangles?

Try it!

SHAPES THAT ARE THE SAME SIZE AND SHAPE ARE CONGRUENT.

How can we find the side lengths of the rectangles?

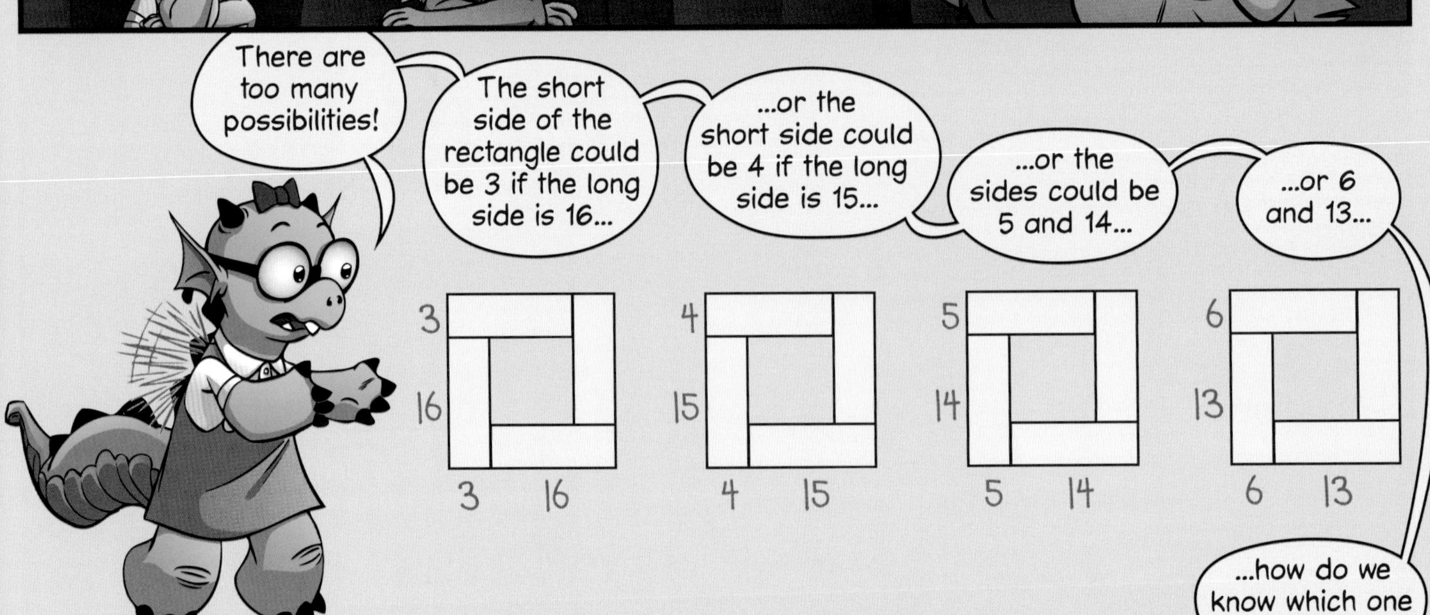

There are too many possibilities!
The short side of the rectangle could be 3 if the long side is 16...
...or the short side could be 4 if the long side is 15...
...or the sides could be 5 and 14...
...or 6 and 13...
3
16
3 16
4
15
4 15
5
14
5 14
6
13
6 13
...how do we know which one to use?

IF YOU'RE STUCK ON A PROBLEM, DO SOMETHING!
TRYING SOME POSSIBLE ANSWERS CAN HELP YOU SEE PATTERNS THAT HELP YOU GET UNSTUCK.

It doesn't matter!
The rectangles you labeled all have the ***same perimeter!***

Find the perimeter of each rectangle Lizzie labeled.

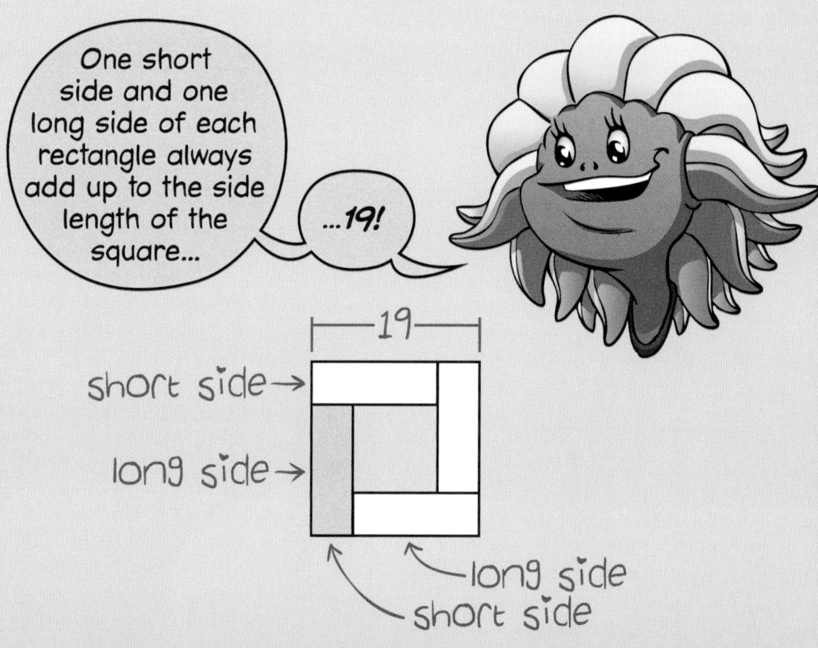

And this one has a perimeter of 15+4+15+4=38.

This one has a perimeter of 14+5+14+5 =38 too!

Each rectangle has two short sides and two long sides...

38!
Correct!

Great Job, Little Monsters!

Today's math meet champions are the Little Monsters of Beast Academy!

Index